Discovering Folk Music

Discovering Folk Music

STEPHANIE P. LEDGIN

FOREWORD BY
GREGG AND EVAN SPIRIDELLIS,
COFOUNDERS, JIBJAB

 PRAEGER

AN IMPRINT OF ABC-CLIO, LLC
Santa Barbara, California • Denver, Colorado • Oxford, England

Front cover: Pete Seeger performing at the Smithsonian Festival of American Folklife (now known as Smithsonian Folklife Festival), Washington DC, June 25, 1982.

Library of Congress Cataloging-in-Publication Data
Ledgin, Stephanie P.
    Discovering folk music / Stephanie P. Ledgin ; foreword by Gregg and Evan Spiridellis.
        p. cm.
    Includes bibliographical references and index.
    ISBN 978-0-275-99387-0 (alk. paper) — ISBN 978-1-57356-771-8 (ebook)
1. Folk music—United States—History and criticism.   I. Title.
    ML3551.L36   2010
    781.62'13—dc22   2009051216

14   13   12   11   10   1   2   3   4   5

This book is also available on the World Wide Web as an eBook.
Visit www.abc-clio.com for details.

Praeger
An Imprint of ABC-CLIO, LLC

ABC-CLIO, LLC
130 Cremona Drive, P.O. Box 1911
Santa Barbara, California 93116-1911

This book is printed on acid-free paper ∞

Manufactured in the United States of America

For Mom,
with love

And for Mary Travers, whose voice was silenced as this book went to press. Her music—that is, the music of Peter, Paul and Mary—was a major influence on my own immersion in folk music. And for Mike Seeger, who also passed away after my manuscript entered production. Mike's enormous talents provided a wealth of knowledge and enjoyment for me, particularly in recent years.

Contents

A photo essay appears after page 88 in this book.

Foreword

My brother and I grew up in the seventies, when folk music was permeating pop culture. We were taught to sing Woody Guthrie's "This Land Is Your Land" everywhere from preschool to summer camp to elementary school. It was—and still is—a staple of childhood in America.

The song, as we knew it, was about love of country and national unity. (We later learned that two of Woody's original verses about the haves and have-nots were lost in the widely popular version.) In 2004, during that year's presidential race, when we decided to make a parody about the country's disunity, "This Land" was at the top of the list of songs for consideration. Comedy is always best when expectations are turned on their head, and there is no piece of music that we knew of that conveyed unity better than the melody of "This Land."

When it came time to craft the lyrics, they just flowed. The song is fun, catchy, familiar, and instantly conveys a sense of Americana. After a couple of rounds polishing the lyrics, we locked down on the folksy photo collage animation style that, together with the song, would help transform our Internet endeavor, JibJab, into an international sensation.

Music is an incredibly powerful art form. Folk art is typically associated with being accessible—anybody with ambition can pick up the tools he or she has at his or her disposal and create it. There is little, if any, polish, just raw creativity. When we created JibJab, we harnessed new forms of media in a way that had never been possible before for folk artists. In a way, we think of ourselves as digital folk artists.

Today, with computers, music creation software, and the Internet, production *and* distribution technology is accessible to everyone. The balance of power in media is shifting from the distributor to the creator. With that, there is no doubt that digital technology will lead to the creation and discovery

of great folk art and folk music that might not otherwise have had a chance
to find an audience; our work certainly wouldn't have.

Just imagine if Woody Guthrie had had the Internet to share his message
and music directly with his audience.

Gregg and Evan Spiridellis
cofounders, JibJab

Preface

Music of many styles was an integral part of my family's history and lifestyle. My paternal forebears operated a music shop in Riga, Latvia. My grandfather was a tap-dancing vaudevillian, while my grandmother is reported to have played folk-style banjo. My mother is a trained classical pianist and violist. Dad likes to tickle the ivories, favoring a range of music from Dvořák to Scott Joplin. And my siblings each sing and/or play music as well. After failing at piano lessons, my lot fell to dancing . . . and to writing about music.

My maternal grandfather used to sing Russian folk songs as he toiled around his garden. I remember well his enthusiastic "ai-da-ukh-nem, ai-da-ukh-nem," as he sang in Russian "The Song of the Volga Boatmen," followed by the World War II movie hit song by Irving Berlin, "Oh, How I Hate to Get Up in the Morning." Speaking of Berlin, how many people are aware that "God Bless America," an alternate anthem we sang in grade school, is not a folk song of an early era in America's history, but in fact was written by Berlin in the 20th century?

In light of this environment, whether I knew it or not, folk music, as far back as I can recall, was always present in my life. Among my earliest childhood recollections are family sing-alongs that would keep my brother and me, and later also my sister, amused as we traveled on long journeys, crisscrossing the country during summer vacations. The station wagon would be packed to capacity, and we would drive from Louisiana to our original home state of New Jersey to visit grandparents, and later from Kansas City, Missouri, back East. There were trips that took us down the Eastern seaboard all the way to Miami Beach and others that took us to the West Coast to Disneyland, with endless hauls across Texas and forays into Mexico. I clearly recall on these many trips my mother enthusiastically leading us in song, such staples as "She'll Be Coming 'Round the Mountain," "Oh! Susanna," "Michael, Row the Boat Ashore," "On Top of Old Smokey," and "I've Been Working on the Railroad."

At home, in addition to a healthy dose of classical music, our "record player," as it was known back then, would spin out Broadway show tunes, Calypso sounds from Harry Belafonte, Cajun music from Jimmy C. Newman, popular numbers from songbirds Edith Piaf and Judy Garland, Yiddish and Hebrew folk songs and dances, and Dixieland jazz from the likes of the Preservation Hall Jazz Band. Occasionally, we would gather around the piano to *Sing Along with Mitch* (Miller), relying on lyric sheets that came with the songbook.

A memorable highlight of our years living in Louisiana was attending a performance by the Philippines National Folk Dance Company, Bayanihan, with its colorful and lively bamboo pole choreography. The show ended with the entire troupe singing "You Are My Sunshine," in tribute to the state's governor, country music's Jimmie Davis.

Meanwhile, the radio offered Tennessee Ernie Ford's "Sixteen Tons," Johnny Horton's "The Battle of New Orleans," and Chubby Checker's new craze, "The Twist." The Everly Brothers harmonized on "Bye, Bye Love," while Bobby Darin cranked out "Mack the Knife," and Jimmy Dean boomed over the airwaves with "Big, Bad John."

Television, too, brought music into our household. When my brother, sister, and I were youngsters, such programs as *Captain Kangaroo, The Howdy Doody Show,* and *The Mickey Mouse Club* all featured various styles of music and dance. But it was the Saturday-morning cartoons that subtly provided perhaps our first introduction to folk music from that medium, with background soundtracks often tapping into such well-known traditional melodies as "Arkansas Traveler," "Turkey in the Straw," and "Irish Washerwoman." Beyond that there was "The Ballad of Davy Crockett," a hit with many a kid, and of course, at the end of each episode on their series, Roy Rogers and Dale Evans rode off harmonizing on "Happy Trails."

As we entered the sixties, folk music popped up more frequently on television and in movies, supplemented by the relatively young homegrown genre known as bluegrass. Music from *The Andy Griffith Show* and its Darling-family episodes, *The Beverly Hillbillies, Bonnie and Clyde,* and *Deliverance* all remain forever etched in our memories.

We were transplanted New Jerseyans living a stone's throw from the Gulf of Mexico, deep in the heart of Dixie, a region infused with music and traditions that intertwined Cajun, Creole, Tex-Mex, country, and more. A family move to the heart of the Midwest introduced into the mix even greater diversity of ethnic cultures, as well as Ozark mountain music that would drift northward. Back in the late fifties and early sixties, genre distinctions seemed nonexistent, or at least I was unaware music could be pegged this or that. It was simply "good music" that infiltrated one's listening receptors.

Fifth grade for me was an eye opener, actually an ear opener. As she led us in a vocal music lesson, my teacher accompanied herself with a many-stringed instrument that caught my attention for its full, flowing, gentle tones produced when strummed. It was an autoharp, and it was this folk instrument that stuck with me for life. I bought my autoharp in 1971 while a freshman in college, an Oscar Schmidt 15-chord style, which I own to this day.

Junior and senior high school had the obligatory square dance sessions during phys ed class, much to our dread back then. We often mocked the music as corny or hillbilly. But there was something about the sound of that fiddle . . .

All this music, regardless of definition or arrangement, was (and remains) part of the American landscape, an unwitting introduction to folk music, alongside and woven into the fabric of popular and classical genres.

I truly do not remember when the phrase "folk music" first entered my vocabulary; simply somewhere along the way I came to know that Pete Seeger, the Weavers, Harry Belafonte, Woody Guthrie, and Paul Robeson were "folk singers." (Robeson was not exclusively folk and Belafonte's repertoire crosses over into other genres as well.) But I do recall that, as I approached my teen years, a period when music becomes more relevant in many an adolescent's life, folk and folk-rock sounds, alongside the pivotal music of the Beatles, moved front and center in my listening tastes.

I was about a half-step behind in age from the inception of what is now referred to as "the folk boom"—the era beginning in the late fifties and stretching into the early sixties—to fully feel its impact, yet I managed to embrace the roots music that is the basis of what is today commonly referred to as folk music. In the sixties' music that I was immersed in—British invasion, folk-rock, and surfer sounds, as well as all the other music I grew up listening to—there seemed to be some tie to folk music, if even a loose one.

Donovan; the Lovin' Spoonful; Peter, Paul and Mary; Brewer and Shipley; Bob Dylan; Nitty Gritty Dirt Band; the Byrds; and so many more great artists contributed to my knowledge and love of folk music. But there is no one exact moment, group, or event that was the impetus to my discovering folk music. For me, it has been and continues to be a lifelong process without end.

I feel very fortunate not only to have been raised in a home and family filled with all kinds of music, but to have stumbled into professional situations that permitted me to work in folk and bluegrass music for more than 35 years. As an editor of a bluegrass magazine, I learned how controversy over genre definitions is in reality a good thing, contributing to its growth. Producing concerts in New York City—including the highly acclaimed Masters of the Folk Violin in which then future bluegrass superstar Alison Krauss was featured—I was handed the challenge of blending genres seamlessly to attract tried-and-true and new audiences alike.

I was proud to be a part of the groundbreaking format, from 1989–1990, of *CityFolk,* as one of its original hosts on WFUV 90.7 FM, public radio in New York City. Radio broadcasting had been my aim when I graduated from college, but those were still the days when women faced obstacles in attaining such goals. And while director of the New Jersey Folk Festival at Rutgers University (coincidentally my alma mater), I perceived the need and introduced into the programming mix a component critical to folk music's future. Along-side authentic practitioners and revival folk artists, "new folk" singer-songwriters were given exposure in order to preserve tradition while encouraging traditions of the future to be heard, thereby expanding musical borders and permitting the creative process to grow.

Discovering Folk Music is my view of the music as I have journeyed along its many paths; it is a guidebook which will allow you to experience it in classic as well as innovative ways. Not a folklorist or other type of academic but a music journalist, I am accustomed to conveying information as well as opining about it. Throughout I encourage an open-mindedness to allow for all concepts and styles that touch upon the parameters of the genre. With this personal ap-proach, *Discovering Folk Music* can be your gateway to discovering a rainbow of music, music made by folks for folks, bringing together a mixed bag of ideas, cultures, and communities.

Space limitations and editorial discretion contributed to keeping this intro-ductory guide focused and expedient, as well as subjective. The perspective from which I have experienced folk music throughout my life was central to the final manuscript. Not every name, famous or otherwise, will be found here. The folk music world is bigger and wider than most of us realize. A housekeep-ing note: Many artists who were or are a part of the broad picture of American folk music are actually Canadian-born. I have not made a point of segregating them or mentioning that fact in some instances.

Folk music is rich in its diversity, drawing from the deep wells of our origins and family heritages, from our country's history often intertwined with that of our bordering neighbors, from our spiritual beliefs and social interactions, and, of course, from our emotions and our passions.

It is my hope that *Discovering Folk Music* will inform you, entertain you, and expand your musical horizons, whether you are 30-something, a baby boomer, a member of the mature crowd, a teenager, or somewhere in between. This book is for you.

I invite you to explore your roots as well as new folk traditions. You will dis-cover there is folk in all of us.

Stephanie P. Ledgin
July 2009

Acknowledgments

It is difficult, if not impossible, to cite every person and place that has played a role in and contributed to the encyclopedia of folk music within my heart and brain. Certainly the largest chunk of my gratitude goes out to the army of colleagues, friends, and family for the educational and supportive roles they have played, not only during the research and writing of this book, but throughout my life and career. This includes the legions of musicians and music business people with whom I have crossed paths personally, "on record" only, or via the printed page, paper or virtual. And it extends to the hundreds of performance spaces, broadcast personalities, and media professionals, among others, who have contributed over the years to the sum total of my knowledge and experience.

Thanks to all the musicians and folk-related personalities who shared their thoughts and time, providing interviews, perspective, and quotes, formal and casual. And to their managers, agents, and press representatives who facilitated, my sincere appreciation as well.

To all those affiliated with the many record labels, large, small, or independent, this book could not have come to fruition without all the audio and/or visual resources sent my way for research. This very long list includes not only label execs and their artists, but more specifically the publicity and marketing people who reach out every day to ensure artists' voices are heard around the world.

My heartfelt gratitude goes to Gregg and Evan Spiridellis for graciously agreeing to take part in this project. Their inspiring, creative use of folk music within their groundbreaking craft, JibJab Media, is awesome.

A particular nod goes to Roger Deitz, talented songwriter-singer-author-friend; he knows why. For special advice, input, and hand-holding, I thank my dad Norm Ledgin, an author in his own right; my brother David Ledgin;

my dear friend Terri Horak; and Judith McCulloh, retired executive editor, University of Illinois Press, whose wisdom and friendship are priceless. Another brother, Alfred Ledgin; niece Calla Jucha; and nephew Eric Ledgin provided interesting under 30/under 20 insight. For opinions shared casually or candidly about various aspects of this book, thank you to countless friends and other family members, way too numerous to list.

Thanks also to Buff Barr at the Hunterdon County Library for assistance in procurement and extended loan of many books used in my research.

Sing Out! editor Mark Moss and his staff, present and past, have provided invaluable support and assistance not just during this project, but over the last couple of decades. Special thanks is due Lee Michael Demsey, Linda Bolton, and Tineke Marburg for facilitation efforts above and beyond; to Cynthia Tannehill Faulk Ryland, daughter of musicologist John Henry Faulk and folk singer Hally Wood, for a warm, insightful conversation about Woody Guthrie; to Rounder's Ken Irwin and my Livingston College music guru Walter O'Brien for technical input; and to Daniel Berger at The Museum of Broadcast Communications Archives and Martin Gostanian of The Paley Center for Media for archival fact-checking; and especially to everyone with whom I interacted/ interviewed informally at the Folk Alliance 2003 conference in Austin and at the NERFA 2007 conference in the Catskills.

Discovering Folk Music took more time to write than originally intended. Without the exceptional patience, faith, and dedication of my editor, Daniel Harmon, along with support staff (editorial, production, marketing, and public relations) at Praeger, ABC-CLIO, and Apex CoVantage, this book could not have come to fruition.

To any and all whom I have inadvertently overlooked in my acknowledgments, my apologies can only substitute for my thanks. With the mountain of information researched and collected for this book, including scores of conversations and interviews, it was impossible to include everything. Rest assured every scrap gathered was integral to the final outcome of *Discovering Folk Music*.

I would be remiss if I did not mention Maybelle, an extraordinary feline who literally was by my side while writing my first two books and who lost her second battle with cancer during the creation of this one; her spirit and quiet courage remain with me and inspire me daily. She was a true folkie cat, immortalized in *Sing Out!* by Roger Deitz in his fall 2006 (volume 50, number 3) RagTag column.

Finally, to my husband, Ted Toskos, who continues to support me unquestioningly in all of my endeavors, I give my everlasting love.

Introduction: Why Folk Music?

January 18, 2009. The Lincoln Memorial, Washington DC. Pete Seeger, just shy of his 90th birthday, accompanied by the iconic Bruce Springsteen, is leading hundreds of thousands of people amassed along the mall in singing "This Land Is Your Land" during the preinaugural concert, guest-of-honor President-elect Barack Obama singing along. Nowhere could the words of Woody Guthrie have been more moving, more inspiring, more meaningful to Americans as we looked toward an unprecedented era in American history.

Folk music. There it was, front and center, on this country's most important stage.

*   *   *

When it was announced in 2006 that Bruce Springsteen was about to release a CD entitled *We Shall Overcome: The Seeger Sessions,* inspired by songs from the repertoire of folk singer-activist Pete Seeger, there were mixed reactions—from both the Springsteen camp and folk music fans. Not surprising was the view some die-hard rock and rollers took, that "The Boss" was selling out, abandoning the music that put him on the global map.

On the other side were in-the-know folk enthusiasts who questioned the choice of material for *The Seeger Sessions* as perhaps not folk enough, politically charged material lacking, a horn section beefing up the punch, and renditions that were more hard-driving than folk music is generally perceived to be. Yet most in the folk community at minimum stood by the project for its quality presentation and arrangements and for, at the very least, providing entrée for nonfolk fans to the genre. In fact, it went on to take home that year's Grammy Award in the Best Traditional Folk album category.

What an interesting—and appropriate—situation for folk music to be in.

In a completely different setting, a media sensation was created by brothers Gregg and Evan Spiridellis, when they offered comic relief during the 2004 election year by portraying presidential candidates John Kerry and George W. Bush in an animated parody based on the well-known alter-anthem of the United States, "This Land Is Your Land." JibJab, their Internet-based venture, was catapulted into the spotlight around the world, with its *This Land* video being viewed on every continent, including Antarctica, as well as on the International Space Station. Seen by millions upon millions by year's end, the spoof led to the JibJab founding brothers being named People of the Year on ABC's *World News Tonight with Peter Jennings*.[1]

Many a child has grown up singing the inspiring folk song, written nearly 50 years ago by Woody Guthrie, whose music laid the groundwork in the mid-20th century for what most of us today identify as folk music. And now "This Land" was being heard, and probably hummed, by countless numbers of people, American and non-American alike, via the JibJab spoof.

What an interesting—and appropriate—place to find folk music.

Just as the success of the music from the 2001 Coen Brothers film *O Brother, Where Art Thou?* propelled bluegrass music into the spotlight, the Springsteen release and the JibJab animation join a number of diverse projects of the last decade involving folk music that have infiltrated the popular culture—and continue to keep folk music relevant, appealing, and growing. Clearly, folk music, thought by some to have given up the ghost to rock music by the end of the sixties, left an imprint that remains a part of American culture. And now in the wake of numerous placements in the public eye and ear, folk music is finding new generations of listeners and resurfacing for those who crave it once again.

In 2000, the film *Songcatcher* set the stage for a broader understanding of our search for our musical roots, and thereby our cultural ones as well. It told the story of a musicologist who relocates to Appalachia just after the turn of the 20th century. There she is astounded to find traditional Irish and Scottish ballads being kept alive in their original form, by ordinary people in their day-to-day lives, as they had been for generations across the pond. She then embarks on "catching," or collecting, the songs for posterity and further study, utilizing a rudimentary recording device. The music was portrayed with an excellent degree of authenticity, tapping the talents of such genuine artists as Hazel Dickens, a leading singer-songwriter in the bluegrass tradition whose West Virginia mining family and community provided impetus for much of her work of the past four-and-a-half decades.

The film shadowed real life. In it we find traces of a number of people and events—the collecting of the Francis Child ballads of England and Scotland during the late 19th century; the gathering of songs by John Jacob Niles in the early 20th century in Appalachia and other Southern regions; song collector Cecil Sharp's quest for English and Scottish ballads throughout Appalachia, also in the early 20th century; and the travels and documentation done by father

---

[1]Jennings died in 2005. ABC has since renamed the program *World News*.

and son folklorists John and Alan Lomax, who captured traditional music not only in rural America but also in diverse lands abroad. Finally, *Songcatcher,* set in North Carolina, depicted the essence of the founding of the nonprofit educational John C. Campbell Folk School, located in Brasstown, North Carolina. Campbell's widow, Olive Dame Campbell, opened the school in 1925 with the focus on "catching" the old mountain ballads as well as on preserving folk handicrafts.

Reading random online fan reviews of this movie was insightful, for they revealed its attraction and reach. *Songcatcher* pulled in newcomers to folk who were taken by the "folksy mountain music," while others renewed a "passion for folk music." Paraphrasing, another stated the music "grew" on him/her, never having encountered such music prior to seeing the film, and going on to say "it's powerful stuff!"[2]

In 2003, spoofmaster Christopher Guest (and co-writer Eugene Levy) gave us the mockumentary film *A Mighty Wind,* an irreverently accurate portrayal of aging sixties' folk stars reuniting for a concert, inspired by the real-life Carnegie Hall spectacular that brought together for a final time the Weavers in 1980 and spawned the documentary *Wasn't That a Time?* The film, while not as enthusiastically embraced as Guest's *This Is Spinal Tap* and others, was often cited for its original music, dead-on re-creations of the sounds that came out of early sixties' folk acts. The actors Harry Shearer, Guest, and Michael McKean, in character as the Folksmen, even sang on the *Late Show with David Letterman* and on *Saturday Night Live,* among other programs. In addition, one number from the movie, "A Kiss at the End of the Rainbow," was nominated for Best Song at that year's Academy Awards and was performed during the broadcast by Mitch and Mickey (actors Eugene Levy and Catherine O'Hara). Folk music was again in the big time. What a great place for it to be.

Legendary director Robert Altman previously had covered a variety of music on film when he turned to the long-running live radio show *A Prairie Home Companion* for the subject of his 2006 project. Earlier, *Nashville* (1975) focused on the country music industry of that metropolis, while *Kansas City* (1996), along with the related documentary *Jazz '34* (1996), spotlighted the Depression-era music of that river city. With real-life host-humorist Garrison Keillor at the helm, *A Prairie Home Companion* starred, among others, Meryl Streep, Lily Tomlin, Woody Harrelson, and Kevin Kline, bringing to movie theaters the potpourri of traditional folk, cowboy, blues, and popular music that has driven the program, nearly continuously, since its inception in 1974.

Bob Dylan made a splash anew in 2008 when he was awarded a special Pulitzer Prize "for his profound impact on popular music and American culture, marked by lyrical compositions of extraordinary poetic power."[3] Revered by many as *the* folksinger of all time and simultaneously followed by legions as

---

[2]http://barnesandnoble.com and http://amazon.com, customer reviews of *Songcatcher* DVD; viewed May 2008.

[3]http://www.pulitzer.org/bycat/Special-Awards-and-Citations.

a megarock artist, Dylan unquestionably provided a cornerstone for today's folk singer-songwriters.

Over the last several years, among notable Dylan-related releases are his autobiographical book, *Chronicles Volume One* (2004); two Grammy Award–winning CDs, *Love and Theft* (2001) and *Modern Times* (2006), both for Best Contemporary Folk Album; famed director Martin Scorsese's epic 2005 PBS documentary *No Direction Home;* the unusual 2007 biopic titled *I'm Not There;* and late 2007's *Other Side of the Mirror: Bob Dylan Live at the Newport Folk Festival 1963–1965.* This last item brings to fans seminal footage from that legendary stage, where over time Dylan morphed before our eyes from acoustic folk singer to plugged-in rock star singing folk songs, creating controversy at that time which, in hindsight, now appears moot.

The iconic cultural magazine *Vanity Fair,* on its November 2007 cover, publicized "The Folk-Music Explosion!" referring to a photo essay, "All Over This Land," by acclaimed photographer Annie Leibovitz, reportedly a "folkie" during her high school days. The spread included history-making stars (Joan Baez, Arlo Guthrie), up-and-comers (Fionn Regan, Ben Kweller), and some whose music is on the outermost fringes of folk (Feist, Devendra Banhart), among others.

Coming full circle, with limited showings in late 2007 and aired on public television in early 2008, *Pete Seeger: The Power of Song* hit the screens. This documentary did more than open the window on the life and times of Seeger, as he approached his nonagenarian decade. By telling Seeger's story, award-winning director Jim Brown succeeded in conveying the essence of folk music, its basic elements, its relevance, its impact, and its staying power.

And while not a folk music project, it spoke volumes when beverage giant Coca-Cola chose to create its own folk song, sung to acoustic guitar and harmonica accompaniment, for a commercial which aired originally during the opening ceremonies of the 2008 Olympics in Beijing. Coke is arguably one of the best-known American products around the world, and it is, at the very least, interesting to note the global company chose American folk music for its marketing message.

Seemingly to attract the broad spectrum of baby boomers to today's 20-ish crowd, Pepsi-Cola, too, turned to folk music, albeit rock-edged, with its "Forever Young" ad, first featured during the 2009 Super Bowl. Bob Dylan was joined digitally by will.i.am singing/rapping Dylan's sixties' anthem for the ages.

THE FOLK IN ALL OF US

So why all this fuss about folk music?

There is folk music in all of us. All of us, our families, derive from diverse heritages. And with our family backgrounds, we bring cultural customs and celebrations, typically with music and/or dance as components of these traditions, handed down from generation to generation, across borders and oceans.

Perhaps you are of Irish descent and spent many a festive occasion at a *ceilidh*, socializing, listening to lively fiddle and accordion, and step dancing to age-old tunes brought to America from across the Atlantic. New York City's annual Puerto Rican Day parade is boasted as one of the country's largest ethnic fetes, with its multitude of colorfully dressed ensembles dancing down Fifth Avenue to a salsa beat. The splendor of India is celebrated each year in communities around the United States with spectacular flair, with musicians and dancers demonstrating time-honored traditions in intricate costumes.

How about the ever popular Oktoberfests that dot the map across the country, with Germanic foodways, drink, and music? The fixin's are souvlaki, gyros, and baklava, washed down with ouzo at many a Greek festival each spring where the entertainment features skilled young folk dancers who step with precision and grace to the bouzouki's melody lines. Polka music is a mainstay in numerous transplanted Eastern European communities throughout the United States, including Czech, Slovak, and Polish, with annual fairs devoted to ethnic pride. The *New York Times* spotlighted one such dance tradition in Nebraska in its limited "America's Music" series, November 27, 2007, edition.

Folk music fits right in with all this cultural pride and exposition. America's folk music is a reflection of the multitude of communities that comprise this land, and therefore contribute to the vast folk music scene.

Along with this, in the last decade a veritable "back-to-roots" sensibility has steadily pervaded our lives. "Natural," "organic," "environmentally-friendly" are all words becoming more common and reflecting a shift in our way of life, our way of thinking. Accompanying this lifestyle attitude are not only baby boomer-era rock songs revived as soundtrack to video advertising, but folk, folk-rock, and kinder, gentler acoustic music pitching goods that range the gamut from pet products to breakfast foods to banks to automobiles. Think of our times in the early 21st century as an older, wiser Woodstock generation, pining to get back to the garden, wanting to share the values that emerged during that era, an integral component of which was folk music.

Forty years after Woodstock, music appears to be taking a reflective look as it forges ahead. Folk music, under the guise of "roots music," "Americana," and other more distinctive folk-related genres, such as blues, traditional country, and bluegrass, is grabbing its fair share of attention in the public eye once again. Amid this exposure is a growing number of high-profile, nonfolk performing artists who are embracing, returning to, or at least giving a nod to folk music.

In 2008, the 50th Annual Grammy Award show was one such testament to this when Levon Helm, a founding member of rock music's the Band, picked up the honor for Best Traditional Folk Album with his release, *Dirt Farmer*. A quintuple encore coup ensued in February 2009 at the 51st Annual Grammy Award show when Led Zeppelin's Robert Plant and bluegrass superstar Alison Krauss took home five Grammy statues for their cross-genre collaboration entitled *Raising Sand*. Not only did the duo capture best album and best record wins, they also covered award territories in country, pop, and contemporary folk/Americana categories.

And when speaking about roots, one can also turn to this nation's history, where music has served as a soundtrack to events since its founding. That soundtrack was exemplified in the 2007 recording *Song of America*. A project initiated by former Attorney General Janet Reno, it features a diverse array of well-known artists from the folk, country, and roots music scenes, offering interpretations of 50 songs that represent this country's past, present, and future.

All these back-to-roots efforts point to the enduring nature of folk music—and that it is not so much a return to folk, but a renewed visibility. Folk music has never disappeared from the map of music. It has always been here and always will be.

In contemporary times, the great era known as the "folk revival" jump-started 50 years ago. Stronger than ever, what makes folk music so durable, so inviting, and, in most cases, so family-friendly? In short, it emanates from the heart, the soul, the brain, the conscience. It is spawned by family, faith, and community. It crosses the great divide of farms and cities, of countries and oceans.

But what is folk music? What is its place in the larger scheme of all music? What is its relevance to our lives and times? And what is *not* folk music?

Let's get on with the journey, because now could not be a better time to discover—or rediscover—folk music.

1

What Is Folk Music?
Beyond "Kumbaya"

In her review of the Tom Hanks–John Candy film *Volunteers,* writer Rita Kempley made reference to "idealistic young Kumbayahoos, who went off to save the Third World," regarding the movie's storyline mocking Peace Corps volunteers (*Washington Post,* August 16, 1985).

During a newscast, while reporting on party unity during the 2008 election year, CNN White House correspondent Suzanne Malveaux commented that "nobody's singing 'Kumbaya' just quite yet" (CNN, June 20, 2008).

Prior to becoming C-SPAN's Director of Communications, political maven Howard Mortman maintained a blog category for three years devoted to "kumbaya moments" on http://extrememortman.com. Political strategist Dan Carol maintains his Web site alias at http://kumbayadammit.com.

Amid postinaugural dust, Keith Olbermann, host of MSNBC's *Countdown,* referred to "kumbaya bipartisanship" on his January 27, 2009, program.

By late 2006, long before the 2008 election, "kumbaya-isms" were so prevalent that they led reporter Jeffrey Weiss to examine the phenomenon in his article "How did 'Kumbaya' become a mocking metaphor?" (*Dallas Morning News,* November 12, 2006).

In turn, Meghan Daum mocked politicos and media types for their sundry kumbaya references in the context of the presidential campaign when she wrote "All Together Now. The History of the Use and Abuse of 'Kumbaya'" in her *Los Angeles Times* op-ed column. She even pondered why we had yet to actually witness a performance of the song, "preferably at an Obama rally," further noting that, for the first time in her career, folk singer Joan Baez had endorsed a political candidate (*Los Angeles Times,* March 29, 2008).

From the sports arena, in a piece regarding discord within baseball's White Sox team, reporter Joe Cowley noted "Expect everyone to . . . all but sing 'Kumbaya,' while holding hands" (*Chicago Sun-Times,* June 3, 2008).

After her much-publicized antics, an online entertainment headline described Britney Spears as "Cucumber Calm–Almost Kumbaya" (*TMZ.com*, January 31, 2008).

A *Loose Parts* cartoon panel depicted a rock guitarist having just finished playing a killer version of "Kumbaya" (*Loose Parts* by Gilpin and Blazek, July 1, 2008).

Do an Internet search for "kumbaya" and hundreds of hits are returned, from usage in the realm of politics, religion, sports, and entertainment to results directly related to this song from more than a century ago.

"Kumbaya." A song from elementary school days and campfire sing-alongs.

"Kumbaya." A song that conjures up ideology of unity or gathering of people for a common cause.

"Kumbaya." A song that symbolizes peace for some, a spiritual beckoning for others.

"Kumbaya." An approximately 100-year-old *folk song* whose precise origins remain unclear but appear by most accounts to derive from, or perhaps were transplanted to, the Georgia Sea Islands, as the word(s) *kum-ba-ya* in the Gullah dialect mean "come by here."

* * *

In March 2008, rather astonishing news was reported. A recording—predating Thomas Edison's first effort by 17 years—was found in a Paris archive. Captured on a device called a phonautograph, the 10-second clip is a *folk song,* the French "Au clair de la lune." The phonautogram was made on April 9, 1860.[1]

Folk music? The oldest recorded "anything," and hence, the oldest recorded piece of music? There must be something pretty special about folk music, or perhaps it was the rock and roll music of its day?

Folk music. What is it? Where does it come from? What does it sound like? Is it new? Is it old? Can anybody play or sing it? Can you dance to it? Is it a fad or is it forever? Folk music. Now, where have I heard that song?

ANCIENT TONES

There are a number of commonly used expressions that have been bandied about for decades when it comes to defining—or attempting to define—folk music. One out-of-print book referred to folk in its title as "more than a song," while a quote that pops up frequently, attributed to influential blues musician Big Bill Broonzy, alternatively to jazz great Louis Armstrong, is that folk music refers to "all songs" because one "never heard no horse sing 'em," or as is sometimes noted, "horses sing none of it."

But there is no straightforward answer or one that academicians alongside legions of folk music fans agree on. Regardless, one can easily imagine the most

[1] Jody Rosen, "Researchers Play Tune Recorded Before Edison," http://nytimes.com, March 27, 2008.

primitive form of music itself as the simple human voice. A sound, a vocalization, a mother cradling her infant, humming or sounding out notes to soothe its crying. Someone whistling or humming random notes while strolling. This for me is the beginning of folk music at its most basic level and the genesis of all music—music made *by* man or woman *for* another person, or at the very least, heard by another person.

Scholarly definition clearly sets its parameters as to what folk music is: that which is handed down, largely by oral or aural tradition, within family or community, and from which its practitioners generally do not derive or seek to realize income. Folk music under this mantle typically has purpose or a message, accompanying life cycle celebrations, spiritual or sacred rituals, or assisting workers in their labor. In this last context, think prison chain gangs, for example, who sing, chant, or clap to maintain rhythm of a repetitive task to toil in unison. Folk music for recreation is exemplified by play-party songs, once popular in rural American communities in particular. Within these parameters, academics typically distinguish folk music usage as being either *secular* or *sacred*.

Regardless of utilitarian role, as folk songs of long ago traveled across many roads, waterways, and generations, it was not unusual for variations in lyrics to occur as they went through regional adaptations to fit local purpose, language translations, or dialect differences in pronunciation.

But let's go back first, before we get to more modern times and what we perceive today as folk music. To understand the roots and development of any genre, we must first examine music from its primal stages. Categories and styles of music represent changes from, variations on, and arrangements of the earliest forms of music, all of which could be referred to as "folk" music, in that the music was being made *by* people *for* people, no matter the context.

The Bible is a great starting point. References abound not only to singers and songs but to dance and musical instruments as well. Regardless of the fact that translations from biblical Hebrew, Aramaic, Greek, or Latin to modern English will render varying interpretations of what a particular instrument might have been most likened to contemporarily, it remains clear that music was integral.

Psalm 150 (the final in the book of Psalms) is a splendid example where many musical instruments, in addition to dance (*makhol*), are delineated, among them (ram's) horn or trumpet (shofar), psaltery or lyre (*nevel*), harp (*kinor*), drum or timbrel (*tof*), stringed instruments (*minim*), and cymbals (*tziltzal*). Experimental musician-composer Ilan Green, best known from the Israeli rock band Tractor's Revenge, recently interpreted long-established research about biblical instruments. He designed and built a collection that includes strummed, plucked, or bowed stringed instruments, "shakers," hand drums, and other percussion instruments. He then assembled a small group of musicians and singers to portray what the music might have sounded like two to three thousand years ago.[2]

[2]A sample of the music, titled "Voices of the Levites," may be viewed and heard at http://www.youtube.com/watch?v=B8_nX-I4jHc.

Looking to another early era, ancient Greece is rich in its history of music and music-making, in both sacred and secular realms. An array of instruments, along with musicians and dancers, is commonly portrayed on treasures from early civilizations.

In 1997, renowned Greek composer Christodoulos Halaris established the Museum of Ancient, Byzantine, and Post-Byzantine Musical Instruments in Thessaloniki, Greece's second-largest city. Here, Halaris recreated with authenticity scores of musical instruments, basing the reproductions on depictions and written descriptions contained in centuries-old artifacts. Musical notation was discovered and used widely in Greece during the seventh century B.C.E., and this, too, was embraced by Halaris as part of the museum project. He organized an orchestra whose musicians perform on the reconstructed instruments, playing works that have survived whole or in fragments from manuscripts dating to the Byzantine period.[3]

More than 200 instruments are displayed in the museum and represent three classes: stringed, wind, and percussion. One easily identifies in modern terms such exquisite examples of original folk instruments, such as harps (*kithara, lyra*), bowed instruments resembling violins (*toxoton*), small guitars and other plucked or strummed instruments (*panduris*), bagpipes (*askavlos*), flutes (*avlos*), and tambourines (*timpanon*). Certainly any number of these instruments and their cousins are recognized today as used regularly and widely not only in American folk music, but in folk cultures across the map.

So in simplistic terms, all music was folk music up until that point in time— within the last couple of centuries—when identifying classifications, or descriptions, were assigned, and all music that remained without a category remained folk music by default.

FOLK MEETS CLASSICAL

Applying this assumption that all music began as folk music, it is interesting to note where it has zigged and zagged along the way to arrive at the 21st-century idea of folk music. You will likely discover that you have already experienced more folk music than you realize. Remember those philharmonic concerts you were dragged to in your school days? Or those fabulous, albeit sometimes corny, Hollywood musicals of the thirties and forties you sit up late into the night watching on cable? Or perhaps it is those family-friendly shows that never really end because they are in constant syndicated rotation? You might be surprised to look back and learn about the folk music or dance incorporated into them. Let's rewind.

Classical music first evolved around the ninth century, distinguished from common music by a more sophisticated form and style. While not referred to

[3]Museum is located at 12-14, Katouni Street, Thessaloniki; telephone 30-2310-555263-6.

as "classical" in the Western hemisphere until the 19th century, it was originally reserved for the higher social and ruling classes, hence, the term "classical." This music went through various incarnations and development during the Medieval, Renaissance, and Baroque eras, taking the shape most like what we identify now as classical around the 16th century.

Medieval music, until written notation came into wide usage, still reflected oral tradition. Troubadours are notable from this time frame for their "courting" love songs. They were composer-poets who maintained that love and music were inseparable. The term "troubadour" today typically connotes folk music.

During the Renaissance and into the Baroque period, music began to develop more complex structures. Twentieth century, street-singing "doo-wop" singers would have been at home during the Renaissance with that era's madrigals, poems set to music, usually for several voice parts, and sung a cappella.

As classical music continued to develop from the 18th century through the first half of the 20th century, composers who clearly borrowed from folk music in at least some of their works can be readily identified. Among them, Beethoven recalled through lively, lilting musical expression his life in the country in his Sixth Symphony, the *Pastoral*. During the second half of the 19th century, Czech composer Bedřich Smetana emerged as founder of Czech nationalist music, with works immersed in Bohemian folk songs and dances. *The Bartered Bride* is perhaps his best known work outside his homeland.

Twenty years his junior, fellow Czech composer Antonin Dvořák was directly influenced by Smetana, under whose direction he played viola in an orchestra. Not only did much of his music reflect the Bohemian as well as Moravian folk sounds, such as in his *Slavonic Dances,* but in his American sojourn in the 1890s, he was so struck by the folk music contributions of African Americans, Native Americans, and the American West's cowboy culture that he borrowed themes and phrases from all three for his Ninth Symphony, titled *From the New World,* and for his String Quartet No. 12 in F, the *American.*

Others who followed the path of incorporating folk music and dance into their compositions as classical music moved into the last century were Charles Ives, who looked to church hymns, patriotic songs, and dance fiddlers, among other inspirations, to create innovative original American music, ahead of its time more than 100 years ago. His contemporary, Hungarian Béla Bartók, was hugely affected by East European folk song—gypsy and village music—readily heard in his compositions. He eventually met up with fellow Hungarian Zoltán Kodály, who instructed him in the methods of collecting and recording authentic folk song material, and the two collaborated thereafter. Both composers are considered among the most significant early ethnomusicologists.

American composer and music critic Virgil Thomson was born in 1890 and raised in Kansas City, Missouri, where he was exposed to Civil War and cowboy songs, early blues, barn-dance music, Baptist hymns, and other folk songs, in addition to popular songs of the day. He went on to study music formally, and the sum of his listening and learning experiences are reflected in his diverse works. Two fine examples are his acclaimed film scores for *The Plow That Broke the Plains* and *Louisiana Story,* for which he was awarded a Pulitzer Prize in 1949.

Decades after its modest success when it first appeared in 1935, folk opera *Porgy and Bess* was finally recognized as one of this country's most pivotal, if not somewhat controversial, operas. Created by brothers George and Ira Gershwin, along with writer DuBose Heyward, the opera breathes life into its African American setting in the Deep South of the early twenties, with its expressive blues and jazz renderings woven into beautiful orchestrations. "Summertime" is one of its best-known pieces. Legendary folk guitarist Doc Watson is among legions of artists from diverse genres who have covered it.

"Beef. It's what's for dinner." Most of you reading this abbreviated advertising line will immediately hear in your subconscious minds the catchy music that accompanies this long-running television and radio commercial. It is likely something you have heard elsewhere on countless occasions as well. The music is "Hoedown" from Aaron Copland's ballet suite *Rodeo,* which derives from several folk and fiddle tunes. Written during a period in American history when the "common man" was central to this country's sociopolitical climate, "Hoedown" was taken from the traditional tune "Bonyparte" (also known as "Bonyparte's Retreat across the Rocky Mountains"), as transcribed in *Our Singing Country* by Ruth Crawford Seeger (Macmillan, 1941) from the playing of Kentucky fiddle player W. M. Stepp. Copland's *Rodeo, Billy the Kid* (with its cowboy songs), and *Appalachian Spring* (incorporating the Shaker hymn "Simple Gifts") are all recognized as quintessentially American epics that capture exquisitely the essence of our country.

Instinctively, we know that what we are hearing is or has some connection to folk music because it is part of the cultural tapestry that reflects the history of the United States. It is a musical expression we have not necessarily been "taught" to identify, yet one with which we have grown up. The music has a certain "feel" about it, a certain color and vibrancy that speaks "American."

FOLK MUSIC GOES TO HOLLYWOOD

Along the same lines, while folk music was finding a place within popular classical settings, Hollywood films also neatly wove folk into the fabric of the occasional story line. Television, too, has often placed folk, blues, and other roots music within programs that were not devoted to music or otherwise related. Here are a few scenes you might recall and, where again, you might not have said to yourself, "Hey, that's folk music," but yet somehow you knew it was.

One of the best-known television series to incorporate folk and fiddle music from time to time was *Little House on the Prairie,* based on the books of writer Laura Ingalls Wilder (1867–1957). Wilder was inspired by her own family's frontier story, taking a cue from actual events and personalities, and for whom music was embedded in 19th-century life. Various segments either made reference to or showed "Pa" playing his fiddle at home or at a local social, where square dancing was typically taking place. One episode features an elderly woman playing autoharp and the singing of such folk songs as "Go Tell Aunt Rhody," "Camptown Races," and "Going to Boston."[4]

The music from this era is considered so important in American history that, in 2005, the Pa's Fiddle Project was established "to pay musical tribute to Laura Ingalls Wilder for her efforts to capture the place that music-making once occupied in the family life of ordinary Americans." To date, the project has produced two CDs, with more in the works, which highlight the music that underscored Wilder's *Little House* books and which provide a window into American pioneering life. One hundred twenty-six songs or tunes are mentioned in the eight books in Wilder's series, covering "parlor songs, stage songs, minstrel show songs, patriotic songs, Scottish and Irish songs, hymns, spirituals, fiddle tunes, singing school songs, play-party songs, folk songs, a Child ballad, broadside ballads, Christmas songs, catches and rounds, cowboy songs, and . . . reference to 'Osage war dances.'"[5]

Prior to the *Little House* years, there was *The Andy Griffith Show*, which not only found Andy strumming a guitar and singing "The Crawdad Song" or "Cindy" but also featured the real-life bluegrass band, the Dillards, as the backwoods, music-playing Darling-family sons, a central role in several episodes. Griffith had already established himself as both a singer and an actor in the mid-fifties with his role in the Elia Kazan film *A Face in the Crowd*. With his folksy style, Griffith continued to introduce television viewers on occasion to folk, gospel, blues, and country music on his later series, *Matlock*.

A great example of Hollywood embracing folk music is the memorable 1939 John Ford film *Stagecoach*, with its original, Oscar-winning score based on American folk music. From the hymn "Shall We Gather at the River?" to the bluesy "Careless Love" to songs by beloved 19th-century composer Stephen (Collins) Foster ("Gentle Annie" and "Jeanie With the Light Brown Hair"), the movie is captivating with its music tie-ins, much as the 2001 Coen Brothers' *O Brother, Where Art Thou?* was—and likely would not have been as successful had it not been for the music. However, it should be noted that many of the works used did not derive from the canon of "authentic" period music, as outlined by academics, those not contemporarily written but handed down by oral tradition; all were utilized to provide color and "flavor" to the story line.

The forties brought to the screen *Meet Me in St. Louis*, set at the turn of the 20th century and starring Judy Garland. In it, we are treated to a scene where party guests dance a lively reel to a revised version of "Skip to My Lou," one of the longest surviving play-party songs from the early days of this country,

---

[4] *Little House on the Prairie*, "If I Should Wake Before I Die," season 1, episode 6.
[5] http://pasfiddle.com.

still sung by children today. The reel is a type of social folk dance that dates to Colonial times, brought to these shores from the Celtic Isles.

The brilliant use of traditional Mexican folk tunes, blended with contemporary classical, jazz, and pop, provides a colorful song and dance backdrop for the 1945 musical *Anchors Aweigh,* which starred Frank Sinatra, Kathryn Grayson, and Gene Kelly. In one memorable scene, Kelly's gracefully adroit dancing takes him through the paces of the traditional "Mexican Hat Dance" ("El jarabe tapatío"), gliding into jazz-infused steps which then segue into an inspired hoedown, ultimately returning to the slow strains of the original tune.

More recently, on the television series *7th Heaven,* the occasional episode during its decade-long run featured a song. One included a guest appearance by folk-pop star Jewel, who sang one of her hit singles, "Good Day." In another, a rousing rendition of "This Land Is Your Land," sung by the Camden family characters, greeted the Reverend and Mrs. Camden upon their return home from a trip abroad. The curtain came down on *7th Heaven* as it bowed out with the Albert E. Brumley gospel song, "I'll Fly Away" and headed into perpetual syndication.

The series finale of *West Wing* (May 14, 2006) closed with an African American blues player offering a rendition on resonator guitar of "America the Beautiful" for the episode's presidential inauguration. And in the 2003 movie *Cold Mountain,* based on the novel by Charles Frazier, we are treated to the moving sounds of sacred harp singing, also called shape-note singing, a traditional form that dates to early 18th-century England and subsequently carried to America.

All of the above are instances where the viewer does not consciously think, "That's folk music." Yet she/he knows it is folk music by the sound and the setting in which it is taking place.

BUT CAN WE DEFINE FOLK?

Now that I have refreshed your memory about folk music that you have likely encountered, let me return to the question at hand—what is folk music? The fact is it can mean different things to different people. Sure, there is the stereotypical "folkie" performer with the acoustic guitar or banjo, often depicted as a leftover hippie in garb and hairstyle, just as "the blues" conjures up images of older black men singing and playing steel guitar or harmonica. And for sure, by and large, folk music is more heavily "acoustic" rather than "electric" in typical instrumentation.

But one can also point to centuries-old oral tradition of West African griots, traveling singers and poets, from whom rap or hip-hop artists are believed to trace their roots and influence. Rap can be viewed as a kind of "street folk," so to speak, addressing relevant social issues, particularly popular and utilized by the generation under 30—African American, Latino, or white. Is rap any less folk than an old ballad from the 1600s?

Rather than limit the scope of folk music set by preconceived notions or restrictive confines applied by folklorists and ethnomusicologists, I prefer to think that folk music for the 21st century should embrace and honor tradition—and simultaneously be permitted to create innovative sounds and establish new traditions.

By offering a framework, I hope to open your world to a variety of folk music that will make you curious to know and hear more. In subsequent chapters, I will lay out a brief history of folk music in the United States. From there, I will point you in the direction of what I will be identifying as the three main branches of today's folk music scene, as we look to the future, while recognizing folk music's vital and vibrant past.

First will be music that is widely recognized and identified as *traditional*, including old folk songs and tunes that either remained and were carried forward with early settlers of this country or were written "in the traditional style." Early country music, such as the vast amount of material captured by the pioneering Carter Family in the first part of the 20th century, contributes heftily to folk repertoire performed today and is treated as traditional. Country blues, including Delta, Piedmont, and "folk" blues, will be touched upon in chapter 2 as a more recent addition to the canon of traditional music, but will not be treated in depth here. See the appendix, "More Folk: Selected Resources," for additional gateways to blues and its practitioners.

The second aspect of the music will zero in on the *folk revival*, reaching back first to its roots in the Depression-era music of Woody Guthrie and those who followed. The relatively short span of time known widely as the "folk boom," which historically began roughly 50 years ago, extending into the sixties, will garner the most attention here, in that this period of folk music constitutes, for the most part, the backbone of all folk music that has evolved since then. Folk musicians who were not "born" into traditional music are typically known as revivalists, those who have adopted and/or adapted traditional, or traditional-style, folk music for performance.

Straddling the traditional and revival worlds is bluegrass music, considered by some a "modern" folk genre, by others an offshoot of country music, albeit recognized by all as its own style. Bluegrass developed in the middle of the 20th century and experienced a great boost in exposure and popularity at the turn of the 21st century. An important player in the folk revival scene, bluegrass will be touched upon in subsequent chapters. For a more in-depth introduction to this American-made music, I recommend my first book, *Homegrown Music: Discovering Bluegrass*. This and numerous other reference materials can be found in "More Folk: Selected Resources."

New folk, which takes its cue largely from the folk revival years, will encompass singer-songwriters and cutting-edge artists whose sound and arrangements often cross over into pop, country, ethnic music, and even rock realms, but whose lyrical bases remain steeped in folk sensibilities. This general movement of new folk artists emerged more prominently in the 1990s and continues to expand.

Common threads run through all of these. Folk music is a living, breathing, ever-changing form; it cannot remain static, because it has a human face and voice. It conveys our family roots, our ethnicities and cultures, and extends to our next generations. It cannot be separated from our lives because folk music is all about our lives, how we live, what we think, our values and ideologies, our joys and sorrows. Folk music is personal, not just as a result of intrinsic characteristics, but as to how it is viewed and perceived by individuals.

Not just for baby boomers, folk music exists for all ages, young, old, and in between. One does not have to look hard or far to find it. It comprises our everyday lives. Folk music inspires, challenges, informs, entertains, plants seeds of change, consoles, calls upon others to act, join in, and be heard. It can be the voice of protest as well as the spirit of hope. Folk music connotes conscience and community. Folk music is an experience in which anyone can participate.

Nora Guthrie is the daughter of Woody Guthrie, the "father of modern folk music." She is the director of the Woody Guthrie Foundation and Archives. I asked Nora, in an e-mail interview of September 30, 2008, to offer her perspective as to the definition of folk music:

> Folk music is the most independent (musical) voice in a society that speaks to that society. It's not restricted to, or by, current or popular thought, style, politics, or religion, although it can speak to any of these. It can be written by an individual, or by a collective. It can last a day, or be timeless.
>
> A good folk song has a uniquely long life expectancy, because it relies on little to exist. It doesn't need anyone's approval; it doesn't need the media, it doesn't need a contract, it doesn't live or die based on the arrangement, the recording, or the performer. It doesn't even need an instrument or a band. All it needs is one human voice (and the spark of truth) to get it started. Its genius is that it can live, and even *thrive*, on very little.

And how did Woody define folk music? Nora pointed to his words displayed on the home page of the official Woody Guthrie Web site:

> A folk song is what's wrong and how to fix it or it could be
> who's hungry and where their mouth is or
> who's out of work and where the job is or
> who's broke and where the money is or
> who's carrying a gun and where the peace is.
>
> —Woody Guthrie[6]

A few decades ago, Pete Seeger took a passage from the book of Ecclesiastes and set it to music. This song sums up perfectly what folk music is, because it speaks to the everyman/woman, to the every occasion of our lives. "Turn, Turn, Turn," the most famous version of which was recorded by folk-rock progenitors the Byrds, states that "To everything there is a season." Folk music provides that voice for every season.

[6]http://woodyguthrie.org.

DAVID BROMBERG: IS IT FOLK?

David Bromberg has been on the music map for more than 40 years, coming of age musically via the vibrant folk scene of Greenwich Village during the sixties. Known for his guitar artistry, eclectic repertoire, and innovativeness—as well as for dynamic onstage spontaneity—Bromberg has never remained wholly within proscribed "folk" parameters. As he points out on his official Web site, he is a "product of blues, country, jazz, folk, and classical music." With that as catalyst, Bromberg has consistently delivered simply some of the most entertaining and top-notch music out there. A skilled violin maker, he continues to tour on a limited basis, preferring to devote most of his time to his retail Violin Shop in Wilmington, Delaware.

I caught up with Bromberg unexpectedly after a show, March 18, 2007, at the Sellersville (Pennsylvania) Theater, in which he performed with avant-garde bluegrass singer Peter Rowan, filling in for ailing guitar virtuoso Tony Rice. On bass that evening was Bob Dylan's longtime sideman, Tony Garnier. Was this performance "folk music"? I would be hard-pressed to put a label on it other than "exceptional."

SPL: We're often asked to define folk music; I'd rather ask what is *not* folk music?

DB: Opera (*laughs heartily*). That's about it!

SPL: Why does folk music matter?

DB: It doesn't matter to everybody. Some people like it; therefore, it matters to them. That's too glib. It's also preservation of culture.

SPL: If you could name just one song that is the epitome of folk music, what would it be?

DB: I have no idea. That's kind of like saying, "Which one of these grains of sand do you like best, what's your favorite snowflake shape?" Even in the United States, when you're talking about folk music, you've got white mountain folk music, black mountain folk music, you've got Piedmont folk music, you've got Delta folk music, you've got so many different kinds. And of course, when you're saying folk music, you include the traditional music of every other country in the world. So you can't epitomize it at all.

2

American Folk Music: A Cultural Mosaic

Folk music has been around for a long, long time. And here in North America, the original folk music is that of the indigenous peoples.

For centuries, the native Indians of the Americas have relied upon oral transmission to pass down their traditions, including music. Their songs and dances were integral to, if not inextricable from, tribal rituals and celebrations. Virtually every aspect of their lives could be expressed through musical form. Drums, rattles, and flutes were the most common instruments. Native American flutes, uniquely constructed with two air chambers, were used widely in courtship. Songs, or vocalizations, as well as melodies could exhibit variations in interpretation; rhythm was typically the most important component, with changes often serving as signals for the singers and dancers of what was to come. The music and dance traditions among the many tribes throughout the Americas were diverse.

Today, much of the Native music performed or contemporaneously composed often blurs the lines, blending traditional sounds with original ones into what has come to be known as New Age music, yet still falls on the folk music continuum. Indigenous Indian music and musicians came into the public eye widely only in the last half-century.

At the forefront, leading the way for others, was Canadian-born Buffy Sainte-Marie (Cree), who first came to prominence in the folk arena during the very early sixties. Writing primarily protest and love songs, many of which were recorded by artists both within and beyond the folk genre, Sainte-Marie penned "Universal Soldier," a hit for Donovan in 1965 and probably her best-known song. She co-wrote the Academy Award–winning "Up Where We Belong" for the film *An Officer and a Gentleman*; it was a number-one hit for Joe Cocker and Jennifer Warnes. Sainte-Marie paved the way for other Indians in the arts, overcoming great discrimination of that era. Her career continues to thrive in various other disciplines, with a focus on her Indian heritage, while limiting concert appearances.

Among the best-known current folk performers is Bill Miller (Mohican), whose original repertoire and world-class flute playing inject soul into the traditional sounds of Native life. His work has been recognized with several Grammy and Nammy (Native American Music) awards. Globally acclaimed Joanne Shenandoah (Iroquois) has taken indigenous American music and blended it artfully with folk, pop, and classical music. She, too, has been recognized with Grammy and Nammy honors.

R. Carlos Nakai (Navajo-Ute), whose name has become synonymous with New Age and world music more so than with folk, is considered the leading American Indian flute player in the world. His innovative cross-cultural explorations have placed indigenous music alongside traditional Japanese, Jewish, and Tibetan, among other ethnic genres.

Meanwhile, back in Colonial times, Europeans were settling in, many from artistically developed areas of the northwest countries. Lively Celtic fiddle tunes and centuries-old English ballads, which related tales of love, family, and life's hardships, were plentiful. Sacred hymns were central to life in the colonies as well.

In addition to violins, or fiddles, it is well known that guitars were present in the colonies and were especially popular as a lady's choice of instruments, in part because of the relatively small size and because they could be played in a proper manner befitting a woman. They were sometimes referred to as "parlor" guitars, because they were often played to entertain suitors in the parlor.

Wooden flutes, both German (played horizontally like modern ones) and English (recorder style), along with harpsichords were also found in the developing Colonial states.[1] The hammered dulcimer was another instrument occasionally heard, probably first introduced here by immigrants from eastern European or Scandinavian countries, as similar multistringed "hammered/struck" instruments were (and still are) found in these ethnic cultures.

But it was not white colonists alone introducing their music to the New World. African slaves brought with them strong and stirring musical sensibilities and traditions, among them—the banjo. Recognized by many as the quintessential "American" instrument, the banjo in reality has its origins in West Africa, where it derived from the *banjar* (also *banjer, bangie, banza*). A de-

---

[1]Interestingly, as this book was going to press, it was reported in the science journal *Nature* (vol. 459, no. 7250) that an approximately 8.5-inch long bone flute was discovered in southwestern Germany, demonstrating the presence of a well-established musical tradition from more than 35,000 years ago. The flute was assembled from 12 pieces of griffon vulture bone and has five holes and a notched end. John Noble Wilford, "Flutes Offer Clues to Stone-Age Music," http://nytimes.com, June 24, 2009.

tailed description of a *banjar* was even noted by Thomas Jefferson in a 1781 journal.[2]

A major characteristic of African song, shared by many of the diverse communities in their homeland, was that of "call-and-response." Often heard in their work songs, for example, this feature carried over into sacred music, when slaves, who were typically converted to Christianity, began to both adopt and contribute to the body of hymns being sung by both whites and blacks. These early spirituals appear to have been documented in the colonies as early as the late 1700s.

While spirituals were primarily sacred songs, they were also used as a secret means of communicating between slaves. Most famously, there were those used to convey messages within the Underground Railroad. For example, "Let Us Break Bread Together on Our Knees" sent a coded call to attend a sunrise meeting to discuss matters at hand, such as escape plans. Spirituals from the 18th and 19th centuries comprise a prominent portion of folk music today.

Popular music of the white colonists and that of the slaves eventually began to meet and merge outside the church. Fiddle became a popular instrument among slaves, who were often drafted to entertain guests in plantation homes or to play for community social dances. After the Civil War, in the late 19th and early 20th centuries, the practice of providing the music for local dances continued, as rural black musicians, known as "songsters," would make the rounds in a regional circuit, playing for both white and black affairs.

Music is mentioned in the writings of our founding fathers and in other Colonial papers. During this era, it was part of the fabric of life, not merely a recreational pastime. "Jaybird Sittin' on a Hickory Limb" was reportedly George Washington's favorite fiddle tune; Thomas Jefferson's was "Grey Eagle." Jefferson, a violinist who practiced daily both popular and classical works, courted wife-to-be Martha Skelton with his skill, often accompanying her harpsichord playing. He even fiddled upon request for Patrick Henry while an overnight guest in Henry's house. As recounted in the April 7, 1947, issue of *Life* magazine in "Thomas Jefferson, Fiddler," by Louis Biancolli, Henry danced a jig to Jefferson's playing, he was so enthralled by it.

Jigs were not all they danced back then. Today's *Dancing with the Stars* craze has nothing on our early settlers. Dancing was something just about everybody did in Colonial times; it was an important component to social and recreational life. Community dances, for example, were where many a young man met his future bride. Country set dancing, a less formal style of English

---

[2]American banjo virtuoso Béla Fleck journeyed to Africa to explore the musical roots of the banjo. The story and music were captured on film in the 2008 release *Throw Down Your Heart*, directed by Sascha Paladino, Fleck's brother. See http://throwdownyourheart.com.

dancing, along with contra dancing were popular. Circle dances were another variation.

You might remember learning "The Virginia Reel" back in elementary or middle school. Taken from the contra dance repertoire, it involves several couples lining up and facing each other to perform the moves across an aisle, a form whose origins are in Scottish longway dancing. This differs from the better known "square dance"—designated as our national folk dance by an act of Congress in 1982—which derived much later, first appearing primarily in West Coast and Canadian regions, but also noted in similar forms, such as *quadrilles,* found in French Canadian provinces as well as in New England. Prior to this, however, the Appalachian square, or "running set," spun off from contra dancing in mountain regions up and down the East Coast.

Slaves, too, had their dances, with characteristic features retained from their African traditions, among them a "bent" stance and accentuated movement of various parts of the body to alternating rhythms. Dance accompanied both spiritual and social music. The Africans' distinctive moves evolved into what became known as "shuffle dances," an example of which is the "buck-and-wing," first popularized in 19th-century minstrel shows. Watch reruns of *The Beverly Hillbillies* and you are sure to catch actor Buddy Ebsen as Jed Clampett doing a variation of a buck-and-wing. Ebsen's fancy footwork could also be seen on film, including alongside Shirley Temple's in *Captain January.*

The buck-and-wing found its counterpart in English clog dances, in which wooden-soled shoes are worn while dancing, to Liverpool and Lancashire hornpipes, for example, as well as in Irish step dances and jigs. Rural folk latched on to a little bit of each, creating a mountain dance style, still done today, called buck dancing or flat footing. Flat footing more closely resembles the black shuffle style, typically done barefoot and with a kind of close-to-the-floor hop-and-shuffle effect. Buck dancing differs in that shoes are worn and there is greater limb movement, often in loose, flailing-like maneuvers; this more forceful beating against the floor in shoes results in more distinctly heard steps. Buck dance or clog steps are also often employed while square dancing. All of these styles contributed directly to the development of modern tap dance.

Dance continues to be a popular activity within folk music circles today. There are hundreds of dance organizations around the country which regularly sponsor traditional English country dancing, contra and square dancing, and clog dance troupes. Many state, county, and 4-H fairs feature square dance groups as well as clogging teams. Professional dance ensembles, such as the internationally acclaimed Footworks Percussive Dance Ensemble, often showcase a variety of styles, some tracing the history of this early American form. While originally buck and clog dancing were primarily done freestyle solo, it should be noted that performance dance executed by current acts is much more stylized and choreographed to showcase intricate artistry and ability. The music and moves are exciting for the dancers and viewers alike, making it difficult not to want to jump up and join in.

Fiery fiddle music is the primary, although not the only, driving force behind square, contra, and clog dancing. And most of the tunes can be traced back to the 18th and 19th centuries, or earlier, from oral tradition. As music continued to blend among black and white communities, pre– and post–Civil War, we heard the exquisitely beautiful union created by banjo and fiddle playing in duet or, alternatively, fiddle backed by acoustic rhythm guitar. This spare sound became the backbone of what we classify today as "old-time music," a passionate, often driving style that is highly danceable. Even the hauntingly sad and slow tunes are generally danceable, albeit typically in slow waltz time.

The term "old-time," which was first applied about 100 years ago, is used to distinguish this music from the more popular forms of country music as well as from bluegrass, created during the mid-1900s by Kentuckian Bill Monroe, considered the "Father of Bluegrass." Old-time reflects the traditional material found in folk music, usually of unknown authorship. Today, a new bank of old-time players often composes tradition-laced tunes that one would be hard-pressed to distinguish from authentically "old" material. The beautiful theme from the PBS documentary series *The Civil War* is one such example of a melody written contemporaneously "in the tradition." "Ashokan Farewell" was penned in 1982 by well-known musician Jay Ungar. In his own words, which illustrate the boundless cross-cultural influences in folk music, Ungar explains on his Web site, "'Ashokan Farewell' was written in the style of a Scottish lament. I sometimes introduce it as, 'a Scottish lament written by a Jewish guy from the Bronx.'"[3]

Old-time music repertoire also comprises the early ballads that were transported to America from across the Atlantic Ocean. These have sustained over time as heartfelt songs that have now been sung for generations throughout Appalachia and by traditional as well as revival folk singers. But by no means are the timeworn ballads only heard within today's old-time music scene. Accompanying instruments used and how a song is arranged and presented determine what label, if any, we assign to a particular aspect of folk music. The old ballads, along with traditional hymns, were—and continue to be—sung by folk revival artists in the latter half of the last century, by country and blues artists, and in pop and rock settings as well.

"Barbara Allen," known by a range of alternate titles, is a ballad that remains as moving today as ever. Believed to date to the 1600s, if not earlier from oral tradition, its origins trace to Scotland. Folk and nonfolk singers alike have recorded it, among them, Joan Baez, Doris Day, John Travolta, Art Garfunkel, and Pete Seeger. It was sung in the film *Songcatcher* in the older, "authentic" mountain style without instrumental accompaniment. To hear "Barbara Allen" and other material sung this way, check out the Digital Library of Appalachia, where Eunice McAlexander of Patrick County, Virginia, for example, renders "Barbara Allen" a cappella (see "More Folk: Selected Resources").

[3]Jay Ungar and Molly Mason Web site, http://jayandmolly.com/ashokanfaq.shtml.

"Barbara Allen" is noted in the Child ballads as number 84. As mentioned in the "Introduction," *Songcatcher* depicts a musicologist's discovery and subsequent collecting, or "catching," of songs from the Celtic Isles that traversed the Atlantic, embedding in hundreds of communities throughout the Appalachians. These songs retained authenticity despite the mileage, passage of time, and errors that resulted from oral transmission and faulty memory. In real life, Francis James Child researched and collected the first seminal work of English and Scottish ballads in America that survived and were found intact. His work, *The English and Scottish Popular Ballads*, known informally as the Child ballads, was published in the late 1800s. With more than 300 songs included, Child laid groundwork for other important musicologists whose work during the last 100 years has been critical to folk music, including that of Cecil Sharp, Olive Dame Campbell, John Jacob Niles, John Lomax and son Alan, Charles Seeger, Archie Green, and Joe Hickerson, among others.

Worship music began to take on a different form in the early 1800s with the spread of camp meetings. These religious camp meetings often would last a week, where two to three thousand people, whites and blacks alike, would gather under large tents to pray. Emotional fervor would build and a new way of delivering spiritual song emerged. Combining lively fiddle tunes with the original melodies of European hymns, a new style of uplifting spirituals was created. African Americans injected their unique influence of call-and-response form, and these highly charged spirituals, historically known as Negro spirituals, became a fundamental component of praise music, ultimately finding its way into the sacred repertoires of both whites and blacks.

The acclaimed Fisk Jubilee Singers of Nashville, Tennessee, were the first to introduce these spirituals to the world, touring the United States and Europe from 1871 to 1875, playing primarily for white audiences, including a performance before England's Queen Victoria. This style and canon of songs became not only the foundation of modern gospel that evolved during the 1900s but also provided much of the soundtrack for the civil rights movement of the last century . . . and has remained an integral part of modern-day folk music as well.

THE MELTING POT GROWS

Meanwhile, as our nation expanded, new immigrants continued to arrive at our shores, bringing Dutch, German, Irish, Italian, Greek, French, Spanish, and numerous others, each carrying with them their Old World languages, customs, traditions . . . and their music. More and more exchange of music took place, resulting in subtle differences in interpretations of many songs. Lyrics would sometimes reflect a personal adaptation or modified story line. Other versions were the result of dialect variations or even misunderstanding of the English language, effecting an inadvertent change in words. All the while, oral tradition remained the most important vehicle for sharing of music.

The proliferation of minstrel shows in the latter half of the 1800s can be considered an unintentional contributor to bringing white and black folk music together. Relying upon the increasingly popular banjo, white performers would appear in blackface, mimicking mannerisms and speech of blacks, as well as their songs and dances. Of course, today these portrayals are looked at in the rearview mirror for their crassness and damaging negative stereotypes. But they provided opportunities for white and black music to coalesce further, laying groundwork for popular American 20th-century genres and adding to the annals of folk music.

Perhaps the best-known and most popular composer of the 19th century was Stephen Collins Foster (1826–1864), whose music is often identified as the essence of American folk music. Various sources continue to argue Foster's intent when he used dialect and words in many of his songs that are now seen as denigrating to blacks, but the fact remains that many survive today as classics from a bygone time in American history. "Oh! Susanna," "Camptown Races," and "Hard Times Come Again No More" are staples, still sung regularly in folk circles and elsewhere.

Pop songstress Carly Simon breathed new life into "Oh! Susanna" when she made the morning television-show rounds performing the song, a cut from her 2007 release, *Into White*. The album is a pop-crossover collection of reimagined old and new folk songs.

JibJab turned to the same song in 2005 for its parody clip, *Big Box Mart*, which spoofed and criticized large retailer Wal-Mart, folk song and social commentary continuing its tradition of joining together to get the message out.

With the frontier opening up and the Civil War effecting changes in this nation, once again folk music experienced new twists and turns, incorporating a variety of blended cultural musics. From cowboy songs in the West to *conjunto* along the northern Mexico border lining the Southwest, to the Cajun music of Louisiana brought there by displaced French colonists, or Acadians, from what is now Nova Scotia, to Scandinavian and Czech communities in the upper Midwest, our folk music continued to embrace and celebrate our diversity.

In recent decades, Tex-Mex *conjunto* has witnessed significant popularity. The style incorporates direct influence from German immigrants who settled during the 1800s in Texas as well as in Monterrey, Mexico, bringing with them the diatonic button accordion and their polka rhythms. Typically, the two most prominent instruments in *conjunto* are the button accordion and the *bajo sexto*, a 12-string guitar. Sometimes called the "father" of *conjunto*, San Antonio's Santiago Jiménez, along with Narciso Martínez from the lower Rio Grande valley, popularized the form in the early 20th century.

Today, it is Flaco Jiménez, Santiago's son, who is world famous as the leading *conjunto* accordion player, although his style now often stretches the outer limits, bending that folk tradition to include other modern genre inflections as well. With several Grammy Awards to his credit, Flaco has taken *conjunto* around the globe and has worked with the diverse likes of Bob Dylan, Ry Cooder, the Rolling Stones, Buck Owens, the Clash, the Chieftains, Emmylou Harris, and Linda Ronstadt.

Linda Ronstadt, whose family came to the Southwest from Germany, settling in Tucson, Arizona, in the late 1800s, has enjoyed an illustrious career that began in folk music with her group, the Stone Poneys, which had a top 20 hit in 1967 with "Different Drum," written by the Monkees' Michael Nesmith. Since then, she has gone on to international acclaim in the realms of rock, country, and traditional Mexican folk music, the last another part of her family heritage.

The Ronstadt family has long been a prestigious musical one. A decade prior to the turn of the 20th century, Linda's grandfather, Federico "Fred" Ronstadt, and several friends formed a band, Club Filarmónico Tucsonense. Music was passed down to his son, Linda's father, who would often play guitar and sing *rancheras,* a traditional Mexican folk style, which was the inspiration behind her Grammy-winning *Canciones de mi Padre* in 1987, followed by *Mas Canciones* in 1991, another Grammy winner. Various Ronstadt family bands have continued to bring siblings together in performance and on record.

Linda's brother Michael Ronstadt and Teodoro "Ted" Ramírez form the core of one of the Southwest's most preeminent folk groups, Santa Cruz River Band. In the late eighties, Ted started the band in Tucson both to celebrate and to present an authentic representation of the multicultural history of the Southwest. An eighth-generation Arizonan, Ted sought to make the Santa Cruz River Band a cultural bridge that would bring together the authentic music and traditions of the region's indigenous people, Mexicans, Asians, and Europeans. The story behind these two performers exemplifies the essence of the cultural mosaic we know as "American" folk music. In an e-mail interview, June 12 and 13, 2009, Ted and Michael explained further the origins of their respective families and how the music and culture translate into Santa Cruz River Band performances. Ted began with a bit of his family's history; then Michael elaborated on his and Linda's musical family background.

TR: The Ramírez family migrated originally from Málaga, Spain, in Andalusia, around 1650. They lived in La Pimería Alta, or New Spain, a region in Mexico now comprised of Sinaloa and Sonora. In 1752, my ancestor Juan Crisostomo Ramírez, a captain in the Spanish Army, served as a linguist and interpreter under Juan Bautista de Anza at the northernmost Spanish outpost, Tubac, New Spain—now known as Tubac, Arizona. My family has lived in the Tubac and Tucson valleys since that time.

MR: My Great-Grandfather Ronstadt came from Germany in the 1840s. He had a great love for music and made sure my grandfather, when he was a young boy, had classical training, which he received mostly in La Paz, Baja California. He had a great love for the music of Mexico, as well as for classical music by German and Italian composers. My grandfather started a band called the Club Filarmónico Tucsonense. He taught the men how to play all of the instruments and wrote out all the scores, as they could not find any music already published for those instruments.

My earliest memories of music were the Mexican records my father would play, operas my grandmother would play on Sunday afternoon, and a bit later, early rock and roll. At about six years of age, I started playing guitar to the Weavers; Peter, Paul and Mary; Michael Cooney; and other folks that would come through the Tucson folk coffeehouses.

SPL: What cultural elements of Southwestern folk music do you embrace in the Santa Cruz River Band?

TR: Language is a big part. We sing songs in English, Spanish, O'odham, and Welsh—European and Indigenous languages. The tradition of expression of positive regional values is equally important. We share stories and songs that relate to the region's historical character, that is to say, the positive values found in Indigenous, Spanish, Mexican, and U.S. traditions and beliefs.

SPL: How much do you draw from your families' ancestries and history in Arizona?

TR: Our entire repertoire reflects our family values, histories, and personally held beliefs and desires. We play songs that have been handed down directly by family members and songs considered essential to the area's culture. They are the songs and stories that our ancestors held—and we continue to hold—dear in their hearts.

SPL: Explain the similarities of Mexican folk music to traditional ballads and fiddle tunes that infiltrated the Appalachians that permit you to seamlessly weave together the styles.

TR: The people of Mexico and Appalachia share many life realities—generally, this is what makes it possible to weave folk styles and cultures together. It is why folks appreciate, and eventually share, each other's music styles. Both regions originally were home to a large indigenous population. Both were influenced by African song styles and rhythms, and both regions are now home to a proud and sometimes clannish immigrant population.

The people live in a geographically rugged and beautiful place, with an abundance of natural resources that they do not control. They preserve the memory of their original homeland with music and poetry. They use music to define themselves and to celebrate the dignity, hope, and resilient ability to overcome hardships, oppression, and poverty.

Both cultures have mastered the creation of cultural joy using folk music and storytelling. The Appalachian and Mexican folk music traditions share the love for intricate rhythmic patterns and time signatures. The blending of a Celtic-styled mountain folk song with African-influenced Mexican rhythm or strumming patterns expands the musical expression without causing conflict for either music tradition. This is a wonderful way for musicians to say hello and share the brotherhood of music.

SPL: Mexican folk music is actually comprised of many forms, unique to each region of Mexico. Which traditions or styles do you embrace primarily in your repertoire?

TR: Being from the United States-Mexico borderland, Santa Cruz River Band does its best to present the region's most popular and influential musical styles. We perform in duo, trio, and quartet configurations, relying upon European and indigenous languages and instruments to capture the authenticity.

From Mexico, we embrace the *son, huapango, ranchera, corrido, cumbia* and *vals* styles. Southwestern folk music is a form of border music performed in a troubadour style. One of my favorite performers is Lydia Mendoza, who was a great "Southwestern Folk Music Troubadour." Her recordings helped keep Mexicans living in the United States connected to their original culture and offered English-speaking audiences a wonderful new folk artist to enjoy. In many ways, Lydia was to the southwestern folk genre what Odetta was to American folk blues.[4]

A couple of states east of Arizona, deep in the heart of the South, the music of the Cajuns, or the Acadians, came to define an entire region of Louisiana. With its signature fiddle and accordion at the helm, Cajun music can be a driving two-step one minute, a slow, tender waltz the next. The Cajun people trace their lineage back to France, from the Breton and Norman regions, eventually settling in what is currently Nova Scotia, Canada. When deported by the English from there in the 1700s, a large contingent ended up in southwestern Louisiana, spilling over also into Texas. They intermarried with the locals, blending and becoming known as Cajuns, derived from the word "Acadian."

Speaking their own distinct language, a hybrid French, the Cajun people are legendary for their mouthwatering, spicy food—and their equally spicy music. Fiddler Michael Doucet, leader of the internationally known group Beausoleil, often points to fiddler Dennis McGee, whose music, along with that of the Balfa Brothers and others, in the early to mid-1900s was among the most in-

---

[4]Mendoza, known as "the Lark of the Border Lands," is credited with popularizing *corridos,* ballads usually sung in waltz time to simple, straightforward accompaniment, when she gained wide recognition in this country from her recordings made in the mid-1900s.

fluential as Cajun music became an ever-increasingly popular form of regional folk music in the 1980s. A vibrant music long on tradition, the vast majority of the Cajun catalog continues to rely heavily upon the original "race" recordings, made roughly between 1929 and 1931.[5]

Sister music to Cajun, also primarily found in Louisiana and east Texas, is the similar zydeco, a bluesier, somewhat countrified style, performed by Creole musicians, with their African American music influences distinguishing its delivery. Also related to Cajun, a quick mention is in order for the increasingly popular Canadian Cape Breton music, which continues to cross our northern border and visit us with such top-flight musicians as fiddler Natalie MacMaster, who is renowned for her step dancing while executing fiery fiddling.

Irish music holds a special place within American folk music. While it is, of course, its own cultural musical expression, it is simultaneously one which most Americans seem to embrace enthusiastically, regardless of individual ethnic or cultural background. Traditional Irish fiddle tunes continue to be heard as backdrop to children's cartoons, the occasional television commercial, and many other American settings. Recently, Folgers Coffee, for example, built one of its commercials around a theme of Irish step dancers. And who doesn't want to dance a jig when we all declare ourselves Irish with the wearing of the green each St. Patrick's Day?

The phenomenal success of *Riverdance* and subsequent similar extravaganzas is proof positive of the draw of this inviting folk music. In addition, it should be noted that the folk revival also brought into the spotlight in this country such Irish and Irish-American performers as Tommy Makem, the Clancy Brothers, Mick Moloney, and the exciting music and dance ensemble Cherish the Ladies. Irish, Scottish, Welsh, and British folk music remain an integral part of today's vibrant folk scene.

Traditional Irish and Scottish tunes figure heavily, as mentioned earlier, in the old-time repertoire as well as in that of bluegrass players. Collaborations between these traditional and modern genre musicians is frequent and well documented, among them, *Down the Old Plank Road: The Nashville Sessions,* a recording by Ireland's the Chieftains with a who's who guest list of bluegrass artists, including Ricky Skaggs, Del McCoury, and Alison Krauss. In the 21st century, cross-pollination of many fiddle and folk traditions is growing in popularity. One unique hybrid takes fiddle tunes from the Scotch-Irish tradition, played in a bluegrass style, and combines them with klezmer music, otherwise known as "Jewish jazz," which originated primarily in eastern Europe in the Middle Ages. More on this growing aspect of folk music in the "No Boundaries" chapter.

Folk songs that evolved during the 1800s preserve for us today a panoramic look back at America as it continued to develop—from sea chanteys and work

[5]Among the earliest recordings, those of early blues and various ethnic folk forms were marketed under the moniker "race" records.

songs to those that reflected the hopes, dreams, and challenges of pioneers heading west to pan for gold, to build a railroad, to work the waterways, or to settle and farm the frontier. "The Erie Canal," "John Henry," and "Sweet Betsy from Pike" are but a few examples of 19th-century America in folk song, all of which remain in our folk songbooks today. Two more key elements contributed significantly to the sound of contemporary folk music as it remains in form today, the blues and early country music, often called hillbilly music.

SINGIN' THE BLUES, COUNTRY-STYLE

Around the turn of the 20th century, early blues music began to surface in rural black communities, by most accounts first in the Mississippi Delta, emerging as a response to the adversity and challenge of a post–Civil War era. It was deeply personal and emotional music, just as expressive as African spirituals, but with a countrified twist as it took shape, an influence of its neighbors in rural areas in particular, where black and white lived in proximity.

This new genre was in itself an idiom, a folk language clearly reflecting lyrical patterns that differed from its Anglo counterparts. Less formal than ballads, blues songs demonstrated looser structure, more story-like—sometimes "talking" story-like—than poetic. As the blues evolved it left more of the rural white influence behind and continued to develop stylistics reflecting both the rural and urban experience of the African American.

Furthermore, as the blues began to widen its reach around the country, it developed distinctive regional variations, including Piedmont blues style, which centered around North Carolina and Virginia populations, Mississippi Delta blues, and those that sprang up along the mighty Mississippi in its river cities including Memphis and St. Louis. It was acoustic guitar–driven music, eventually to be joined by slide guitar and harmonica as identifying hallmarks.

Delta blues were among the first recordings made in the early 20th century, part of the catalog of race records mentioned previously. It was a pivotal time for music because of the advent of these commercial records, which brought music right into people's homes. "Hillbilly" string bands and old-time fiddlers were also highly popular among record producers, including the entrepreneurial Ralph Peer, who was later responsible for the success of some of the most important artists of the early 1900s.

The introduction and availability of records, along with the beginning of regular radio broadcasting, changed the face of musical America forever. Musicians could now be brought right into one's living room on record or live via the radio. As a result of these technological advances, white and black music could be distributed and shared widely, further mixing styles that first met face-to-face two to three hundred years prior.

One of the earliest radio programs to bring folk music into homes across the country was the forerunner to the *Grand Ole Opry*, first aired in 1925, with the permanent name change taking place in 1927. Its producers wanted to present music of the common people—folk music, hillbilly music, string bands, and harmonica players. It did not begin as the country music show we know it as today; rather, references were often made to its folk music programming. At various times in its history, one could hear the program open with "It's Grand Ole Opry time, another big folk music show." And before Nashville—from where it still airs live each weekend—began to call itself the "country music capital," Opry announcers would refer to its broadcast city as "the nation's folk music capital."

In 1927, the historic Bristol, Tennessee, recording sessions took place. In the studio was the "Singing Brakeman" Jimmie Rodgers, also known as the "Blue Yodeler," along with the Carter Family—A. P. Carter, his wife Sara, and her cousin Maybelle, who was married to A. P.'s brother—from southwestern Virginia. For their repertoire, A. P. Carter would go out and comb the countryside for songs, "collecting" them from friends and strangers alike, songs that had been around and handed down for generations. No one knows to this day which among the some 300 songs copyrighted by A. P. were originals versus those he collected, adopted, or adapted from hymns and other sources.

The enormous body of work popularized by the Carter Family in the 20th century continues to sustain the folk, bluegrass, country, gospel, and pop catalogs. Many will recognize "Will the Circle Be Unbroken," "Wildwood Flower," with "Mother" Maybelle's distinctive guitar style or autoharp accompaniment, or "Keep on the Sunnyside," featured, for example, in the Coen Brothers' film, *O Brother, Where Art Thou?*

In recent history, many readers will recognize the connection between the Carter Family and June Carter Cash, wife of Johnny Cash, whose life was portrayed in the highly acclaimed 2005 film *Walk the Line*, in which Reese Witherspoon gave her Oscar-winning performance as June. June was the daughter of Maybelle and she often revisited the music of her family in concert and on record. Her final recordings were in fact those of her family on *Wildwood Flower* (Dualtone 1142), made only a few months prior to her 2003 death.

There are few people today who can say they spent time with and got to know one of American folk music's most influential figures. Bill Clifton did just that with A. P. Carter. Clifton, a performer whose career dates to the early fifties, was especially instrumental in bringing American folk and bluegrass music to countries far beyond U.S. borders. He organized folk clubs throughout Europe and expanded audiences in the Pacific region as well. His long out-of-print *150 Old-Time Folk and Gospel Songs*, first published in the fifties, was in its day one of the most sought after songbooks. Clifton was also one of the driving forces behind a reinvigorated Newport Folk Festival in 1963 during the still booming, but soon to falter, folk era.

As an ambassador of American folk music around the world, Clifton commented recently: "For me, folk music is the music which has been passed from generation-to-generation across all the cultures of the world. *Contemporary music* is just that! It may, *at some future time,* be part of the folk tradition." He continues to be actively engaged in folk and bluegrass music and shared these snapshot memories—and lessons learned—from A. P. Carter, conveyed via written correspondence, December 6, 2008, from his home in Mendota, Virginia.

> From the moment I first came to know the music of the Carter Family, at age fourteen, I sensed that A. P. Carter, his wife Sara, and his sister-in-law Maybelle, were extraordinarily gifted people. The simplicity of their music and the beauty and honesty of the lyrics/stories contained within the three minutes available on a 78rpm record stood head and shoulders above the popular music that served the radio-listeners in the 1940s.
>
> By the time that I was eighteen—and involved in singing and playing my way through thirty minutes of air time weekday mornings on local radio in Charlottesville, Virginia—I had found and bought a couple dozen records by the Carters and knew a lot more about each of them. A. P. was a man that I knew I had to find, as I was absolutely sure that he could teach me what I would need to know if I wanted to earn my living as a performing artist. Somehow it never even crossed my mind that he would consider the importance of an eighteen-year-old boy as unworthy of his attention.
>
> From the moment we met each other, and despite the nearly forty-year difference in our ages, we communicated on the same wave-length. He taught me a great deal about humility, about honesty, and about the sadness as well as the joy that had come to him through music. Not so much in words, but through the way he conducted his personal life.
>
> We had picked up the mail and we were back in A. P.'s own little store as he opened an envelope from BMI.[6] (It contained) a royalty check for approximately $120 made out to him personally, since almost all of the Carter Family's recorded works were attributed to him as writer. He turned to me and said, "Bill, can we go up to Weber City to the bank? I need to cash this check and get checks made out to Sara and Maybelle." We made that trip, and he divided the money into three equal parts and mailed checks to both Sara and Maybelle. It was a lesson about honesty that spoke to me.
>
> "Ownership" of songs is completely legitimate whether you write the song yourself or not. This came to light on a day that I asked a question of A. P. that (folklorist) Archie Green had beseeched me to ask him. Archie was writing his book, *Only a Miner,* and he wanted to know the origin of the Carter Family song "Coal Miner's Blues." I rarely asked A. P. questions of any kind; his daughter, Janette, would remark years later: "That's why Daddy told you so much—'cause you never asked him anything . . . and he wanted you to know." A. P. said he got the song from "some fellow up in Wise . . . I gave him $5 for it." So I learned that the craft of songwriting was like any other commodity. People use their wits

[6]Broadcast Music, Inc., is an entity that collects license fees on behalf of songwriters, composers, and music publishers and distributes them as royalties to those members whose works have been performed.

to get the money needed for life's necessities—and negotiating a sale for a song was no different than negotiating a sale for this year's tobacco crop, or an oil painting on canvas.

As America headed into the Depression era, the pieces of the multicultural mosaic were in place for what would emerge as the foundation of the folk revival movement. And beyond that time, no American genre today can separate itself from some traceable folk roots that merged with novel arrangements and stylings in its development. Most notably, rock and roll directly derives from a confluence of folk, blues, and country music. In the next chapter, we will take a look at how folk music came into vogue and helped shape the music of the latter half of the 20th century. Later we will examine its continued relevance in American music and life in the 21st century.

AMERICA SINGS ITS HISTORY

Numerous CDs exist by artists in a variety of genres, including folk, which tell America's story in songs. One recent project has received particular attention because of who conceived the idea for it. Former United States Attorney General Janet Reno had heard a number of folk songs which depicted in detail key times in America's history. From this she envisioned a recording that would include folk songs representative of all of America's past, from its founding to the present. Reno conveyed her vision to her nephew-in-law, performer/songwriter Ed Pettersen, whose own music straddles folk, blues, country, and other rootsy forms. The result, about a decade later, was *Song of America*, produced by Pettersen and released in 2007. Ed provided further insight in an e-mail interview, June 13, 2008.

SPL: How did you narrow down the selection of material to the 50 cuts you chose for *Song of America*?

EP: It was almost impossible! We chose from over 1500 songs, some of which I had been collecting since I was a kid, but we decided to keep it to three CDs. It could have easily been 10! Ten years ago, Janet Reno drew up 25 eras in American history for me on a piece of paper when the project was first conceived. That was our template and curiously ended up being almost exactly what Deane Root from the University of Pittsburgh and the Center for American Music gave us. She's one smart lady! Anyway, David Macias and I then cajoled and argued about the songs based on those lists until we felt we had a fair and substantive representation of our history that had two songs for each era. It just coincidentally ended up being 50 songs. It wasn't exactly intended to represent 50 states, but it was a happy accident, you might say.

SPL: Was the *Song of America* project envisioned to become part of the history curriculum in schools across the country?

EP: That was the original plan. Ms. Reno's idea when she challenged me to do this was that the collection could inspire students to want to learn more about history. Professor Root has devised a teaching guide which includes all of the songs from *Song of America,* the lyrics, and a history lesson describing why the songs were written and why they are important to our history as a nation. The basic idea is that each day, or once a week, a teacher can play a song from the CD, maybe involve the class in singing and playing a song, and then discuss it via questions provided in the guide. All proceeds from *Song of America* go to this purpose as well as to help the Folk Alliance International and the *Sing Out!* music archive, where I found tremendous materials to start me on this journey. It was a lot of work, but a wonderful ride.

AMERICA'S HISTORY ON RECORD:
A RANDOM SAMPLING

The Arkansas Traveler: Music from Little House on the Prairie [various artists] (Pa's Fiddle PFA01)

Beautiful Dreamer: The Songs of Stephen Foster [various artists] (Emergent Music)

Andrew Calhoun and Campground. *Bound to Go. Folk Songs & Spirituals* (Waterbug 83)

Anne Enslow and Ridley Enslow.

   A Musical Journey in the Footsteps of Lewis & Clark (Enslow Publishers 9780766032873, ages 11+)

   Music for Abraham Lincoln: Campaign Songs, Civil War Tunes, Laments for a President (Enslow Publishers 9780766036352, ages 11+)

   Music of the American Colonies (Enslow Publishers 9780766022 393, ages 11+)

Kim and Reggie Harris. *Steal Away. Songs of the Underground Railroad* (Appelseed 1022)

Sparky and Rhonda Rucker. *The Blue and Gray in Black and White* (Flying Fish 611)

Linda Russell. *The Good Old Colony Days: 18th Century Folk Music* (http://lindarussellmusic.com)

Daniel Slosberg. *Pierre Cruzatte: A Musical Journey Along the Lewis &
   Clark Trail* (Native Ground 940)

Song of America [various artists] (31 Tigers/Split Rock 20654)

This Is My America [various artists] (http://thisismyamerica.com)

200 Years of American Heritage in Song [various artists] (CMH 1787)

Chris Vallillo. *Abraham Lincoln in Song* (Gin Ridge 1009)

3

Folk Revival: 50 Years On

You could listen to his songs and actually learn how to live.

—Bob Dylan, referring to Woody Guthrie[1]

Woody Guthrie, born in 1912 in Okemah, Oklahoma, was the second child of musically inclined parents. His father, Charles, was a cowboy, among other jobs, and he would teach his son Western songs, Indian songs, and Scottish folk songs, while his Kansas-born mother, Nora Belle, passed along her musical influences as well. Woody came of age as the Depression took hold; with a propensity for rambling and the once oil-boom town of Okemah dried up, he set out, settling in the Texas panhandle. There he married, had three children, and made his first foray into music, founding the Corn Cob Trio and later the Pampa Junior Chamber of Commerce Band.

But in 1935, the Great Plains states were hit by a historic dust storm, sending Woody and thousands of other out-of-work, poverty-stricken people West in search of work and food. Eventually making it to California in 1937, he secured a job singing on radio station KFVD in Los Angeles, where he gained his first taste of notoriety. Singing traditional songs and original ones, he simultaneously brought entertainment and inspiration to displaced "Okies" and others living in migrant camps. It was through these efforts that Woody's "social voice"—as an advocate for truth, fairness, and justice—began to emerge and to be heard. It would be his trademark and his legacy.

The urge to keep moving landed him in New York City in 1940, where he recorded his first album of all original material, *Dust Bowl Ballads.* There, too, historical musical associations that would affect the future of folk music began

[1] *No Direction Home: Bob Dylan,* directed by Martin Scorsese, 2005.

to form. During the forties, Woody met, performed, and recorded with many of the folk and blues singers who are now recognized, along with Woody, as the foundation of the folk revival movement.

Among them was Huddie Ledbetter, born in the 1880s in Louisiana. Fascinated by music from the age of two, he became known widely as Lead Belly (often documented as Leadbelly). By the age of 14, he was already a popular musician, proficient on several instruments, including his Stella guitar, which earned him the nickname "King of the 12-String Guitar." He traveled the Southwest working in the cotton fields or laying railroad tracks when not performing his music. But his charismatic way with the ladies led to trouble, and it was during a second stint in prison that folklorists John and Alan Lomax happened upon him, while they were at Angola Farm Prison in Louisiana making field recordings of prison songs.

By the early forties, Lead Belly was resettled in New York City, where he joined up with other performers, including Josh White, Sonny Terry, Brownie McGhee, and Woody Guthrie. White was already established as a blues and folk artist but had received a particular boost in his career in 1940 when he acted alongside the legendary Paul Robeson in *John Henry*, White in the role of musician Blind Lemon Jefferson. Robeson, already acclaimed as an actor and singer—and considered by many an early bridge between mainstream fine art and folk music—would frequently include in his concerts a selection of protest music and international folk songs, in addition to spirituals. By the late 1940s, he would also become one of the most prominent entertainers targeted by government scrutiny symbolized by the approaching McCarthy hearings—hearings which would effectively alter the folk music map forever.

In 1948 Lead Belly recorded what was later compiled and released in 1953 as *The Last Sessions*, a definitive showcase of the depth and breadth of his music, which included prison songs, field songs, children's songs, and others in the folk and blues realms. This unique performer's life was cut short by Lou Gehrig's disease; he died on December 6, 1949.

More than 500 songs comprised Lead Belly's vast catalog, among his best known "Midnight Special," "Cotton Fields," "Boll Weevil," "Kisses Sweeter Than Wine," and "Rock Island Line," to name a few. Perhaps most significant of all his songs was "Goodnight Irene," as it was to be a key player in the folk revival, still simmering at the time of Lead Belly's death.

Influential blues singer-songwriters Sonny Terry and Brownie McGhee first met in 1939, performing and recording together off and on from the early forties until Sonny's death in 1986. Brownie passed away in 1996. Both were Southern-born sons of music-minded families. The blind Terry was known for his expressive harmonica playing; McGhee, although adept on other instruments, primarily for his guitar abilities. Like Josh White, they, too, appeared on Broadway, performing as strolling blues singers in the mid-fifties in *Cat on a Hot Tin Roof*. This broader audience opened doors to more concert and festival gigs in the ensuing years.

Another singer on the New York scene was Burl Ives, the son of Illinois farmers whose English-Irish family provided extensive exposure to old-time songs. Burl showed great talent and was a gifted banjo player as a youngster. He first performed before he was even old enough to attend school, at a soldiers' reunion, standing on a makeshift stage of planks under a cottonwood tree. Starting out as an actor in summer stock, then appearing in several Broadway roles, he simultaneously pursued music, performing at the Village Vanguard. Soon Ives landed his own radio program, *The Wayfaring Stranger,* a moniker that stuck with him and which was used as the title of his 1948 biography. While the minstrel-derived "Blue Tail Fly" remains one of his most popular as a children's folk song, Ives was also notable for his bawdy ones, which were not usually permitted to be sung in public during that era. Burl's distinctive, warmly inviting voice and innate performing ability led Pulitzer Prize–winning poet-writer Carl Sandburg to dub him "the best ballad singer of them all."

The son of renowned musicologist Charles Seeger and musician Constance Seeger, Pete Seeger received something of an accidental baptism in folk music by virtue of exposure to his father's work. In 1935 at the age of 16, Pete, already a tenor banjo player, accompanied his father to a square dance festival in Asheville, North Carolina. There he heard the five-string banjo played, old-time style—and he immediately fell for the lure of its sound, far different than the popular music associated with tenor banjo. This set him on a course that kept him from his original plan to be a journalist. Instead, he worked for Alan Lomax, absorbing more and more about authentic folk music from recordings and field trips. It was probably inevitable that he would meet Woody Guthrie, and within four or five years, he had. He took to the road with Guthrie for awhile, before continuing on his own to explore and develop his music.

In the early forties, Pete Seeger, Lee Hays, and Millard Lampell had been joined by Woody Guthrie and others mentioned above in a fluctuating group of artists that eventually performed under the name Almanac Singers. This loosely knit ensemble went around singing in support of largely left-wing social causes, such as union organizing, peace, and anti-Fascism. Guthrie's original songs became essential to the Almanac Singers' repertoire. The Almanac Singers were a forerunner, in part, of a later group that would break folk music out of the shadows and propel the music of Lead Belly, Woody Guthrie, and others into the American songbook forever.

By late 1945, Seeger and about two dozen other like-minded individuals got together and decided there needed to be a national organization to share their progressive-leaning songs and ideologies. People's Songs, Inc., was born. Newsletters were published and a couple of books as well. To help publicize what People's Songs was all about, the hootenanny came to be. The idea was to bring as many folk singers together for one big concert. The first one was held at Irving Plaza in New York City in 1947. Hootenannies became highly popular later in the fifties and early sixties, and have remained part of the folk fabric since that time. A hootenanny even takes place in the Oscar-winning 1963 film, *Lilies of the Field* starring Sidney Poitier.

But People's Songs couldn't sustain and closed up shop by 1949. However, the idea stuck, was reworked, and in May 1950 the first issue of *Sing Out!* magazine was published. Celebrating 60 years in 2010, *Sing Out!* magazine remains the most important print/digital publication for folk song and folk music. See the appendix, "More Folk: Selected Resources," for further info about *Sing Out!*

FROM WOODY TO THE WEAVERS

The stage was set for changes coming down the pike for folk music and its practitioners. During World War II, Guthrie served in both the merchant marine and the army. During this time, he composed hundreds of songs to rally the troops and others to express his anti-Fascism sentiments; most notable from this body of work, "The Sinking of the Reuben James." In the mid-1940s, Guthrie divorced and remarried. His second wife was dancer Marjorie (Greenblatt) Mazia, with whom he had four children, Cathy (who died at age four in a tragic home fire), Arlo, Joady, and Nora Lee.

By the late forties, the first signs of the disease Huntington's chorea,[2] which would claim the life of one of America's greatest 20th-century songwriters, began to rear its ugly head, visiting upon Woody erratic, sometimes violent, behavior and moods. Once again his family broke up, Guthrie moving and traveling about with a young folk singing protégé, Ramblin' Jack Elliott. Elliott, the son of a Jewish doctor from Brooklyn, became known as the "last of the singing cowboys." He later would befriend and mentor a young Bob Dylan.

By the early to mid-fifties, Woody would find himself in and out of hospitals and mental institutions, ultimately receiving the correct diagnosis of Huntington's. He deteriorated through the end of the fifties and into the sixties, losing his health, abilities, and talents, and remaining in hospital for his final years. There he was visited and entertained by the younger generation who would eventually find their immortal places in folk music, among them, Bob Dylan, Phil Ochs, Joan Baez, and the Greenbriar Boys, along with such friends and colleagues as Pete Seeger, Sonny Terry, Brownie McGhee, and his former wife Marjorie.

Woody Guthrie finally succumbed on October 3, 1967. He left behind some 3,000 song lyrics, among other creative works, now housed in the Woody

---

[2]Now known as Huntington's Disease (HD), it is a rare, incurable, degenerative brain disorder that is hereditary. It was later determined that Guthrie's mother had died from it as well. Little was known about it 50 years ago; therefore, institutionalization rather than hospitalization was the norm at that time. After Woody's death, it was Marjorie Guthrie who organized the forerunner to the Huntington's Disease Society of America. See http://hdsa.org.

Guthrie Archives in New York City. Among his posthumous honors are the Lifetime Achievement Award from The Recording Academy (1999) and induction into the Songwriters Hall of Fame (1970) and into the Rock and Roll Hall of Fame and Museum (1988). The same year Woody was inducted into the Rock Hall, Lead Belly and Bob Dylan were as well. Woody Guthrie was not only the spirit of America at a turning point in this nation's time; he gave America spirit in his songs.

In contrast to the Almanac Singers' loose structure, or lack thereof, Pete Seeger and Lee Hays in 1948 discussed putting together a more concrete, regular group that could hone its skills into a cohesive, solid sound, one that could give a fuller voice and depth to the songs of Lead Belly and others of the same vernacular. They found their complements in Fred Hellerman and Ronnie Gilbert, and eventually settled on the name, the Weavers.

Not looking to be a commercial group, the Weavers hosted hootenannies and played for local events, but found themselves nearly broke by late 1949. Then came the break that would help catapult them to the top of the charts. They landed a gig at the Village Vanguard, where folk, blues, and jazz were the fare and where Lead Belly, Josh White, and Burl Ives had all performed. In other words, it was *the* place to be seen and heard.

At first their audiences were not plentiful. But then Alan Lomax brought Carl Sandburg to hear them. It was Sandburg's remark—"When I hear America singing, the Weavers are there"—that drew media attention, and, consequently, bigger crowds to hear them, leading to enough of a buzz that the Weavers soon found themselves with a recording contract. In May 1950 they cut their first record, "Tzena, Tzena, Tzena," an Israeli folk song, backed by Lead Belly's "Goodnight Irene." Within weeks, the Weavers were at the top of the pop charts with both songs. This was followed by more hits, including "On Top of Old Smoky," "Wimoweh," and "So Long, It's Been Good to Know You," this last written by Woody Guthrie.

But just as fast as success was coming to the Weavers, obstacles jumped in the way as well. The Cold War was generating cold shoulders toward left-wing performers. A television show was offered, and then quickly rescinded, when Pete's name showed up in a right-wing publication, insinuating he was a Communist.

By 1953 the Weavers took a sabbatical, returning to the stage for a sold-out reunion concert at Carnegie Hall during the 1955 Christmas season. A tug-of-war within the group pitted the now age-old argument of commercialism's place within folk music against its social and political roles. Seeger left the group in 1957, reportedly due to his objections over the Weavers' singing for a cigarette commercial. He filmed the commercial, then resigned, replaced by Erik Darling, a member of the Tarriers, the first folk trio to place a hit single on the *Billboard* pop charts.

The Weavers continued performing through a couple more personnel changes, held two nights of Carnegie Hall shows in 1963 in celebration of

15 years, and then disbanded shortly thereafter. A momentous final concert brought the original four together in 1980—less than a year before Lee Hays died—at Carnegie Hall, an occasion around which the documentary *Wasn't That a Time?* was filmed. Released in 1982, this film—the story of the Weavers—was the springboard for the Christopher Guest–Eugene Levy 2003 mockumentary, *A Mighty Wind.*

Today, the legacy of the Weavers lives on in a unique way, providing a glimpse into the music and history of this seminal folk group—and how their music resonates in today's world, just as it did 50 to 60 years ago. The Work o' the Weavers is a quartet that faithfully reproduces in concert and on recordings the original arrangements of the Weavers' songs, taking the music across the United States. The group is comprised of seasoned singer-musicians David Bernz (banjo), James Durst (guitar), Martha Sandefer (vocals), and bassist Mark Murphy.

McCarthy and his cronies played a role that was simultaneously both an impediment to and a furtherance of folk music. Pete Seeger, called before the House Un-American Activities Committee in 1955, was blacklisted and closed out of many a public performance opportunity on stage and on television. But he found an audience in children and in college students, singing at camps and on campuses around the country, thereby planting the seeds for a new generation of "folkies" who would carry the music forward into the era that would become known as the folk boom.

While many confine the "folk revival" era to that commonly recognized as the period from the late 1950s stretching midway into the sixties, in reality public attitude toward folk music had already been changing since the first part of the 20th century, when radio and recordings enabled hillbilly, blues, and early country music, that is, authentic folk music, to be more accessible to a larger audience across the United States. In effect, it was being revived by these new mediums with the interest in the music that this exposure initiated.

When Woody Guthrie began writing original songs, sometimes to old, traditional melodies, and folk music began to bloom all over with performers such as Lead Belly, Seeger, and others, this was essentially phase two of this earlier expansion of folk awareness and the impetus for modern folk music as we know it today. The so-called folk boom years, then, were more like the culmination of a slow, gradual rise in the popularity of folk music, boosted further by the 1952 release of the seminal *Anthology of American Folk Music.* This collection showcased early 20th-century, authentic rural musicians and reinforced interest in traditional music in tandem with topical folk music.

When Woody Guthrie died, he left behind more than just songs. He willed to America the foundation of modern folk music, a new contextual wrap for old music with contemporary relevance. And it was Pete Seeger who took up the mantle to lead in the preservation of Woody's songs alongside traditional ballads and to merge them into a contemporary notebook of folk music, accessible and inviting to all.

Many others in the 1950s gave voice and color to the broad spectrum of folk music. Two women, significant for their lasting imprint upon folk, blue-grass, and other acoustic blends, were Jean Ritchie and Ola Belle Reed, whose music reflects the traditions of their home places. Ola Belle Reed, who settled with her family in northern Maryland, was an unusual singer of the old ballads from her native North Carolina. Her original compositions resonated with her heartfelt philosophies and have entered the encyclopedia of folk songs, em-braced by artists in many camps. She accompanied herself on frailing banjo, employing a rather unique, inimitable playing style. While she performed throughout the fifties and into the eighties, recognition for her music came late in life, primarily in the last decade of her career. Her song "High on the Moun-tain"[3] was most notably a hit for country music star Marty Stuart, and, along with others from her pen, has been recorded by many.

Ola Belle was such a revered, influential figure, that young artists have pro-moted her music vigorously in recent years. The group Ollabelle, anchored by Amy Helm—daughter of rock music's Levon Helm of the Band who, in the traditional folk category, took home a 2007 Grammy for his back-to-roots *Dirt Farmer*—is carrying on her important old-time traditions and heartfelt songs. The Demolition String Band devoted *Where The Wild, Wild Flowers Grow: The Songs Of Ola Belle Reed* to her music, and an annual festival now takes place each August near Ola Belle's birthplace in Ashe County, North Carolina.

Kentucky is one of several states that fall within the great expanse of the Appalachian Mountain Range and where music is inextricably part of its living history, its soul. Kentucky's—and America's—first lady of folk, octogenarian Jean Ritchie has carried the music of her family and home place around the world since the mid-1940s. Her repertoire covers a full range of life's joys and tragedies, from retelling of ballads that crossed the Atlantic Ocean to home-grown original compositions.

Jean was born in 1922 in Viper, Kentucky, where she and her siblings learned songs from oral tradition. After completing college with a degree in social work and moving to New York City, she became active in the local folk doings. She met and recorded for Alan Lomax, and Jean also appeared on the then new radio program *Folksong Festival* whose host was fellow folk singer, Os-car Brand (and with whom she has remained a frequent performing colleague ever since). In 1952, she earned a Fulbright scholarship for a year of study abroad, researching in Ireland and the British Isles the music of her ancestral origin.

As the fifties grew into the sixties and beyond, Jean continued to be a fix-ture on the burgeoning folk music scene, recording and appearing at festivals around the country, laying important groundwork for the furtherance of folk

[3]Sometimes noted as "High on a Mountain" or "High on a Mountain Top."

and roots music. Many of her compositions, as well as her renditions of traditional ballads, have become folk song staples. Her "The L&N Don't Stop Here Anymore" has been recorded widely, by artists including contemporary folk stylist Michelle Shocked and country music's Johnny and June Carter Cash. Linda Ronstadt, Dolly Parton, and Emmylou Harris covered "My Dear Companion" on their all-acoustic *Trio* project in 1987.

There is no pretense in a Jean Ritchie performance. She is genuine and humble, while delivering eloquently the timeworn music that is woven into the fabric of her life. Her distinctive a cappella singing commands notice with its quietude. Unassuming and graceful, strumming her trademark dulcimer on her lap, Jean is captivating, at home singing for an intimate library audience or in a space as magnificent as Carnegie Hall.

Jean was recognized by the National Endowment for the Arts in 2002 with a National Heritage Fellowship. Often called the "Mother of Folk," Jean reflected on her music and her life in music, sharing these thoughts in an e-mail communication on September 19, 2008.

> Music has been much with me all my years; it has not been "my life," but an inseparable accompaniment to it. From being rocked and sung to as a baby in Mom's, Dad's, and sisters' and brothers' arms, to listening to my father's dulcimer ringing, being cradled in the porch swing, joining with the family's voices on soft summer evenings, "singing the moon up"—from all that to the present—making the old and the subtly changing music with friends, as first a mother and now as a tottering old lady, the old songs and the musical strings have kept me company. Indispensable company—I could not have made it through without them.
>
> Life without music, and especially that of my family and my Kentucky mountains and streams, would have been, I feel, pedestrian and without magic and joy. I have never tried to be a famous singer or even a well-known musician—just have needed those remembered scenes, a dulcimer strumming, and my small voice to keep my memories alive, and pass them on, for the joy that is in them. If I have helped anyone, soothed anyone, given smiles or blessed tears to those in need of them, inspired anyone to look for and find his/her own music, quietened a restless crowd to listen in wonder to a soft song—or excited and pleased them into clapping and singing a play-party song with me, I can go happily when my time is up. . . . And if they all keep honoring the old songs, and passing them along to their young ones, I will have done a little good in the world.
>
> How corny this sounds! But sometimes a little corn is good for one—and all!

Harry Belafonte is known to all as singer, actor, civil rights activist, and humanitarian. He was first appointed a UNICEF Goodwill Ambassador in 1987 and, now in his eighties, continues in that role. Belafonte first came to prominence on the theater stage in the 1950s, quickly adding to his storied career as a folk singer, with emphasis on the Calypso music—his signature sound—of his Jamaican heritage. He recorded and released "The Banana Boat Song" just after the Tarriers charted near the top with their single. But it is Belafonte's resonant opening phrase "Day-O, Day-O . . ." that audiences around the world recognize. *Calypso,* Belafonte's third album, was the first in history to top the million-copies-sold mark. Its success contributed to industry standards that laid the groundwork for the Grammy Awards.

In addition to being the first African American to win an Emmy Award, for his 1959 music special *Tonight with Harry Belafonte,* the multitalented performer was responsible for introducing important non-American folk artists to this country, including South Africa's Miriam Makeba and Nana Mouskouri from Greece. In 1994 he was awarded the National Medal of Arts, one of this nation's highest honors. Songs in his extensive repertoire known globally include "The Jamaica Farewell," "Matilda," "Man Smart (Woman Smarter)," "Shenandoah," and "All My Trials."

Called the "Voice of the Civil Rights Movement," Odetta had a most awe-inspiring voice. Trained for opera, she went into theater, then turned to folk music in 1950. She has been referred to as a "stunningly original" performer. Her vocal style derived from an extraordinary ability to merge deeply rooted African American traditional music with modern, urban sounds. Artists as diverse as Joan Baez, Janis Joplin, Bob Dylan, and Joan Armatrading cite her as inspiration.

An American icon, Odetta was referenced in the original screenplay of *Hairspray,* a 1988 comedy film by John Waters. She appeared in the Emmy Award–winning 1974 television film *The Autobiography of Miss Jane Pittman.* Following the attacks of September 11, 2001, it was her voice that sang out later that week on the *Late Show with David Letterman,* performing such inspirational numbers as "We Shall Overcome," "This Little Light of Mine," and "Amazing Grace." Odetta received the Library of Congress Living Legend Award in 2003 and before that, the National Medal of Arts, awarded by President Bill Clinton in 1999. She had been anticipating her participation in inaugural activities for President Barack Obama when she passed away on December 2, 2008.

ALL OVER THIS LAND

While New York City's Greenwich Village is universally thought of as "folk central," it was by no means the only metropolis that spawned important music, music-makers, or music happenings. Urban college cities were prime stomping grounds for folkies about to come of age and break out, among them Philadelphia, Bloomington (Indiana), Berkeley and Los Angeles in California, Cambridge and Boston (Massachusetts), and Chicago. Chicago, for example, had a lively, growing community, enough so that in December 1957, the Old Town School of Folk Music opened its doors. Its initial offerings were guitar and banjo instruction, folk dancing, sing-alongs, and concerts by the biggest names of the day. Then in 1961, the University of Chicago Folklore Society began hosting the annual University of Chicago Folk Festival. Both the Old Town School and the festival are as vibrant as ever today.

A number of events set in motion what is looked back on as the "folk revival" or "folk boom" era, sometimes jokingly referred to as "the great folk scare." And it was the West Coast where, in 1957, three college students reconfigured an already established group and formed the Kingston Trio. With hallmark three-part harmonies as tightly synced as a precision drill team, the Kingston Trio blazed onto the national scene with their recording of the ballad "Tom Dooley." The song went gold when it hit number one in 1958—*and that is considered the official shot heard 'round the world for popular folk music.*

At the first annual Grammy Awards, the song won Best Country and Western Performance; by the following year's second Grammy Awards show, a performance category for folk was added, and again the Kingston Trio took home the prize, this time for *The Kingston Trio at Large* album. The threesome followed up with such memorable hits as "M.T.A." and Pete Seeger's "Where Have All the Flowers Gone," a protest song adopted by anti–Vietnam War activists.

Other West Coast artists of similar style and ilk as the Kingston Trio to emerge or gain recognition from this climate included the Limeliters, who for three years sang the "Things Go Better with Coke" jingle, which became a national hit. The Chad Mitchell Trio, whose sound was similar to other trios, but who included songs with social conscience in its repertoire, such as "The John Birch Society," was the first to record, but unfortunately not to release, a Bob Dylan song, "Blowin' in the Wind." Peter, Paul and Mary had the home run on that one.

In California, the Smothers Brothers combined folk music with silly humor and topical satire. They recorded several successful albums in rapid succession, leading to a television show, which did not do well in its original form. A second version, *Smothers Brothers Comedy Hour*, allowed Pete Seeger in 1967 his first post-McCarthy era network appearance, one that was not without controversy until he was permitted to sing "Waist Deep in the Big Muddy" on a later appearance. Comic actor Steve Martin famously relied on his banjo as an integral part of his stand-up routines early in his career. He released his first banjo CD, *The Crow*, to critical acclaim in 2009, then embarked on his first-ever tour as a musician, playing to a sold-out house at Carnegie Hall.

Noel Paul Stookey of Peter, Paul and Mary began his career on the East Coast with a combination of folk and comedy and carried his delightfully funny monologues with him into the trio repertory. The offbeat humor of Allan Sherman used to light up television variety shows in the 1960s; his album *My Son, the Folk Singer*, was just one of his recordings. A former writer for *Saturday Night Live* and *Late Night with David Letterman*, Andy Breckman was a regular on the New York City folk circuit during the late seventies and early eighties. His songs are unique, if not weirdly memorable, and dangerously funny. "Don't Get Killed" has been suggested as a theme song for the Big Apple, and

"Railroad Bill" has been covered by many. Breckman is the creator and executive producer of USA Network's *Monk*.

Bruce "Utah" Phillips did a lot traveling around with his music. He described himself as the "Golden Voice of the Great Southwest." Few could spin stories and sing songs as humorously or as genuinely as he. Many of his originals have been recorded by such artists as Emmylou Harris, Ani DiFranco, Joan Baez, Tom Waits, and Waylon Jennings. Among his best-loved songs are "Goodnight Loving Trail," "Green Rolling Hills of West Virginia," and "Rock Salt and Nails." His audience spanned across the United States, Canada, and throughout Europe. Utah passed away in May 2008. His long-time friend and colleague Rosalie Sorrels paid tribute when she recorded and released *Strangers in Another Country: The Songs of Bruce "Utah" Phillips* after his death. The CD is a treasure trove of lesser known, rarely performed works by Phillips.

Meanwhile, on the East Coast the folk temperature was rising. Although living and performing in the Boston area in 1959, Joan Baez had landed a two-week stint at The Gate of Horn nightclub in Chicago, where she met folk singers Odetta and Bob Gibson. Gibson invited her to join him in his set at the upcoming Newport Folk Festival. A fixture at the legendary Club 47 (now Passim Folk Music and Cultural Center) in Cambridge, Baez became the talk of the town and the festival as a result of this unscheduled, by invitation, appearance—an appearance that established Baez as the rising talent she quickly became—and a festival that would push into high gear the folk revival, jump-started by the success of the Kingston Trio.

July 11 and 12, 1959, the first Newport Folk Festival was held. The owner of Boston jazz club Storyville, George Wein, who previously had put the Newport Jazz Festival on the map, was intrigued by the hot folk doings emanating from the Cambridge folk clubs across the river. He hired impresario Albert Grossman, with assistance from an army of other folk music heavy-hitters, to produce what became the second volley of shots which firmly rooted the folk music revival. This booming era for folk music, which managed to blend its traditional roots with modern-day troubadours and trumpeters of social conscience, would continue with fervor until a certain mop-headed quartet from Liverpool would change the face of music forever.

Joan Baez was invited to return to the second Newport Folk Festival the following year for her first solo appearance. The year 1960 also saw her New York City concert debut and the recording of her first album, which was met with enormous success. In 1961, at Gerdes Folk City in New York's Greenwich Village, Joan met Bob Dylan for the first time, when he appeared there as the opening act for bluesman John Lee Hooker. Embarking on her first-ever national concert tour that same year, Joan Baez, by November 23, 1962, was the cover story in *Time* magazine.

In 1963 Baez headlined the Newport Folk Festival. That same year, leading a much-publicized artist boycott, she refused to appear on ABC TV's *Hootenanny* for not scheduling the venerable Pete Seeger. The program, which had begun its year-and-a-half run that spring, showcased folk, country, gospel, and jazz artists, along with stand-up comedians.

Half a dozen years prior, in 1956, Baez attended a lecture by the young Martin Luther King, Jr., indoctrinating her in the rhetoric of civil rights and nonviolence. In August 1963, Baez sang "We Shall Overcome" before an estimated quarter million people at the pivotal Civil Rights March on Washington DC, where Dr. King delivered his "I Have a Dream" speech. Other prominent folk artists that participated before this historic gathering included Odetta, Harry Belafonte, Bob Dylan, and Peter, Paul and Mary, along with gospel great Mahalia Jackson.

The mention of the 1963 March on Washington DC brings clearly into the picture folk music's role and its relationship to social causes and activism. On November 10, 2007, at the Northeast Regional Folk Alliance Conference held in Monticello, New York, I had the opportunity for a brief interview with folk singer-teacher-activist Kim Harris, who with her husband Reggie has been touring and recording for 30 years. We talked about people singing together and how to get people singing. Kim offered these comments:

> When people sing together in the room, the air changes. It just literally changes. There's a way that it just brings people together, either laughing or crying or just feeling like you're part of something bigger than yourself. And that is really wonderful. . . . When we were young, we can remember seeing on TV, or if we were a part of it, actually being there, when people were rallying and getting together and trying to change things. Music was a very big part of that. These days, most of the rallies I attend are all speeches, no music. Or if there is music, music is relegated to the night after the rally in a concert. So there doesn't seem to be that *remembering* that the music wasn't just entertainment in between the speeches. The singing together was bringing people together, motivating them, inspiring them, maybe calling them in to do something that they were too scared to do. People have forgotten that.
>
> What I talked about on stage was having courses about how to choose a song for a rally—what are good songs to sing, how can you be a song leader. There are some real specific skills. For many of the people in the modern civil rights (years), they knew those skills because in their churches, they were using those skills in the church context anyway. And so it was easy to say, "Well, we're out rallying, so let's sing.". . . If someone is not trained in that way . . . they don't know how to invite people to sing. They don't know how to keep it going. . . . Just like any other thing, there really is a skill to being a song leader. That's the kind of thing that I'm working to teach people.

A confluence of events and artists continued to build and strengthen the burgeoning folk revival landscape. Back in Cambridge, Tom Rush had been a Harvard student in the early sixties. There he became a fixture on the folk club circuit. He cut his teeth performing at Club 47, a venue that brought to its stage many legends from whom he would learn. Rush's repertoire seamlessly incorporated folk, blues, and country, each delivered in a rich baritone voice. By the time he graduated from college, he had already released two albums.

Rush is remembered best for his 1968 *The Circle Game,* on which he featured Joni Mitchell's "Urge for Going," in addition to the title cut, another Mitchell composition, covered by Joni later on record, and by such others as Harry Belafonte, Buffy Sainte-Marie, Ian and Sylvia, and Maureen McGovern. Songs by two notable singer-songwriters, James Taylor and Jackson Browne—like Mitchell, waiting in the wings for their stars to shine—were also included on the LP.

The recording contained Rush's "No Regrets," which remains his most popular composition, renditions of which have been recorded by Emmylou Harris, Olivia Newton-John, and Belafonte, among others. *The Circle Game* was later referenced as the starting point for a demarcation in folk music, when a greater number of contemporary singer-songwriters were finding their voices and gaining exposure, overshadowing the more traditional singers and players of the folk revival era, faded by this point in time. In 2009 Rush released *What I Know,* his first studio album in 35 years.

Canadian-born Joni Mitchell was arguably one of the most important songwriters to gain exposure from Cambridge-rooted folk performers (and others), Rush among them. While she herself went on to record and become an entertainer of the highest caliber, it is her songs that remain the focal point of her extraordinary talent. "Both Sides Now" has been recorded 645 times, according to jonimitchell.com, a fan-maintained Web site. Most famously, Judy Collins took the masterpiece to the top of the charts and copped a 1968 Grammy for it. Collins has also covered Joni's "Michael from Mountains," included along with "Both Sides Now" on her 1968 *Wildflowers* album; "Chelsea Morning," found on *Living* from 1971; and "That Song about the Midway," a cut on the 2005 release *Portrait of an American Girl.*

"Big Yellow Taxi," Mitchell's second most recorded song, is probably among her most played on "oldies but goodies" radio. From her third album, *Ladies of the Canyon,* it heralded a shift in some of her folk material to more of a folk-pop arena. The 1973 *Dylan* included a version, cut by Bob some years earlier, but which had not been released previously.

But the one song that remains an anthem for a generation is Joni Mitchell's "Woodstock," popularized by Crosby, Stills, Nash and Young, but also recorded with a slower, more introspective arrangement by the songwriter herself and included on the *Ladies of the Canyon* release, along with "The Circle Game." In addition to her music, Mitchell is an accomplished painter and dancer. A few years ago she collaborated with the Canadian Alberta Ballet on *The Fiddle and the Drum.*

Club 47 was a wellspring of talent. In addition to Rush, Baez, and others having graced its stage, Bill Staines is another among those enduring figures. In 1975 he captured the National Yodeling Championship at the Kerrville Folk Festival. Bill's repertory cuts a wide swath across the map of folk music, and includes not only his originals but traditional folk tunes and contemporary country ballads, spiced with humor that sneaks up on you. He has recorded two dozen projects—his most recent is *Old Dogs*—and his scores of memorable songs have been published in many a songbook. Nanci Griffith; Jerry Jeff Walker; Peter, Paul and Mary; and Glen Yarborough are but a few who have brought Bill's songs to audiences across the country. His most endearing song, perhaps, is "Roseville Fair," given a delicate treatment by Griffith on her 1988 record, *One Fair Summer Evening*.

Other important early contributors on both sides of the Charles River to the folk notebook and to the growing bluegrass genre were, among others, Jim Rooney, Eric Von Schmidt, Peter Rowan, Fiddlin' Tex Logan, and Jim Kweskin. Kweskin led a brief revival of jug band music, first popular in the early 20th century. With a five-year run in the 1960s, the Jim Kweskin Jug Band graduated among its alumni such notables as songstress Maria Muldaur, bluegrass banjo innovator Bill "Brad" Keith, and fiddler Richard Greene. Jug band music, which evolved out of vaudeville-era urban black string-band musicians, particularly in river cities, mixes Dixieland jazz, ragtime, and blues. Typical instruments utilized include jugs of all shapes and sizes, ukulele, kazoo, washboard, spoons, and washtub bass. Among active jug bands is an ensemble offshoot of a jug band class at Chicago's Old Town School of Folk Music, the Hump Night Thumpers. First formed in 1965 and still going strong is New Jersey's Dirdy Birdies Jug Band, while Minneapolis boasts its Como Avenue Jug Band.

Few singers have been immortalized in song, let alone while they are still walking this earth. Judy Collins stands, not so much a cut above but, more accurately, a cut from a different cloth among the bolts of fabric that comprise folk music. She was a child-prodigy pianist, growing up in Denver after a move from her birthplace of Seattle, Washington, then to Los Angeles. When she embraced folk music as a teenager, Collins was keenly aware of the depth of its lyrical form, looking at it from the classical literature viewpoint. She maintained this approach as she developed as a folk artist.

Although she is also a songwriter, her legacy is that of song interpreter. Collins took an early piece, "Thirsty Boots," by prolific songwriter Eric Andersen, and captured its poetic beauty on her 1965 LP, *Fifth Album*. In addition to "Both Sides Now" mentioned earlier, Leonard Cohen's "Suzanne," which Collins recorded in 1966 on *In My Life*, demonstrated her extraordinary insight in putting across a beautifully constructed composition and making it her own. Crosby, Stills and Nash paid her talent and beauty the highest tribute in "Suite: Judy Blue Eyes," written by Stills and famously performed at Woodstock, and which was the opening cut on the trio's debut album.

DYLAN BLOWS IN

The names Peter, Paul and Mary are all but synonymous with folk music, protest songs, and the sixties, all rolled into one. The trio debuted officially in late 1961 at the Bitter End in New York City's Greenwich Village. From the start, their impressive, ever-expanding catalog of material embraced social and political issues, while not ignoring the lighter side of life, including songs for children and for grownup kids alike. Significantly, Peter, Paul and Mary bridged the two worlds of "authentic" traditional folk song with that of timely, topical compositions, succeeding not only artistically but commercially.

Their first album, *Peter, Paul and Mary,* released in May 1962, contained two huge hits, "If I Had a Hammer" and "Lemon Tree," sending the LP straight to number one on the *Billboard* charts. Less than a year later, they released *Moving,* which featured another memorable song, "Puff the Magic Dragon." That recording hit number two, while the trio's third project, *In the Wind,* again captured the number-one spot upon its release toward the end of 1963. For a time, all three albums were in the top 20 of the album charts.

August 28, 1963, found Peter, Paul and Mary at the center of the March on Washington. Images continue to be shown today in historical film clips of their powerfully delivered "If I Had a Hammer" and their emotion-filled "Blowin' in the Wind," forever placing these two songs into the annals of antiwar literature.

For the record, some of their most popular songs, in addition to those already mentioned, include "Early Mornin' Rain," "Day Is Done," "One Kind Favor," "Leavin' on a Jet Plane," "Single Girl," "Car-Car," "I Dig Rock & Roll Music," "Wedding Song (There Is Love)," and "The Times They Are a-Changin.'"

Some 50 years later, the music of Peter, Paul and Mary—as a group and in their individual efforts—is still relevant, vibrant, and carrying forward the times. During the near half-century they toured and recorded, they amassed numerous gold and platinum records, Grammy Awards, and other important achievements in both music and humanitarian issues. But the most significant mark of their long and storied career is the intrinsic way in which they changed folk music—and how folk music, in turn, continues to impact life in America.

Mary Travers passed away September 16, 2009, from the side effects of a chemotherapy treatment after successfully battling leukemia. Peter Yarrow and Noel Paul Stookey continue to keep the flame and music alive in their work together and individually.

When a young, determined Bob Dylan arrived in New York City in early 1961, leaving behind Minnesota and his given name—Robert Zimmerman— no one could have imagined the impact his music and lyrics would have on popular music, let alone folk music. But there were hints early on, recognized or intuited by some, including Joan Baez who befriended him after meeting him that year at Gerdes Folk City, and Robert Shelton, longtime critic for the *New York Times.* He wrote in his September 29, 1961, review of the 20-year old Dylan's gig at Gerdes, that Dylan's "highly personalized approach toward folk song is still evolving" and that he had the "the mark of originality and inspiration."[4]

[4]Robert Shelton, "Bob Dylan: A Distinctive Folk-Song Stylist; 20-Year-Old Singer Is Bright New Face at Gerde's Club. Greenbriar Boys Are Also on Bill With Bluegrass Music," *New York Times,* September 29, 1961.

Dylan has cited variously a number of different influences on his work, style, and stage manner, including Woody Guthrie, Muddy Waters, Jimmie Rodgers, and actor-comedian Charlie Chaplin. In Scorsese's docu-bio *No Direction Home: Bob Dylan,* he relates how the "strange incantation" in the way 1950s' crooner Johnny Ray vocalized left an impression. Ray, who was partially deaf, had difficulty phrasing words as a result of his hearing loss, from which he developed an unusual way of delivering a song.

Before Dylan became successful, there was a family—just an ordinary, typical American family of folk singer–photographer enthusiasts—that would provide Dylan with food and a place to stay on a regular basis whenever he would be in upstate New York for a gig. The Alper family was deeply rooted in the sociopolitical folk scene. Jackie Alper was folk singer Jackie Gibson before marrying photographer Joe Alper. Jackie, in fact, had been the one who first introduced Ronnie Gilbert of the Weavers to folk music, bringing Ronnie, then 16, into her folk group, the Priority Ramblers.

By the time young Dylan arrived on the East Coast, the Alper family was living in Schenectady, New York, helping run the now legendary folk club Caffè Lena in nearby Saratoga Springs. The Alper family son, George, recently collected some of his father's candid shots of Dylan—on stage and off, including in the Alper home—and published a photo essay book, *Bob Dylan: Through the Eyes of Joe Alper.*[5] George was only a child when these shots were taken, but as a child of "folkies," his memory of Dylan is an interesting glimpse from a unique perspective. He shared these recollections on August 16, 2008, at the Philadelphia Folk Festival.

> I absolutely loved him from the (first) moment. I mean, even though I was three or four years old, I remember listening to his music. Remember, that wasn't even my first exposure, being a son of a folk musician-rabble rouser from way back, I was constantly exposed to (folk music). I went to the Fiddler Beers Festivals two or three times a year at Fox Hollow. I went to (Caffè) Lena's every Friday or Saturday night, even though I was a little kid. Fell asleep on a cot in what they called the dressing room, a makeshift dressing room which was the pantry. I would be put to bed listening to the strains of Pat Sky or Dave Van Ronk or Pete (Seeger) or Dylan.
>
> That was my world. I didn't realize until very recently how incredibly special my upbringing was, even though it was incredibly normal for me. I mean, doesn't everybody hang out with musicians and have people traipsing in and out of their homes!? Doesn't everybody have people recording albums in their living room!?

Dylan released his debut recording in early 1962, after which his songwriting became more plentiful and more focused on social and political issues. Such originals as "Blowin' in the Wind" and "A Hard Rain's a-Gonna Fall," for example, went far beyond simple poetic ballads. The complexity and intricacy of

[5]http://dylanbook.com, 2008.

his lyrics quickly began to evolve; he could boil down a book's worth of words into an extraordinarily crafted song. His songs started getting published in *Broadside,* a recently founded topical song magazine that quickly became influential on the folk song front.

After a short tour abroad, Dylan finally gave his first major solo concert at Town Hall in New York City in April 1963, which began to draw attention from the media. His second album, *The Freewheelin' Bob Dylan,* came out shortly after that, bringing with it even more positive press and coinciding with Peter, Paul and Mary's release of the single, "Blowin' in the Wind." He then became the big draw for that year's Newport Folk Festival, considered the most prestigious of contemporary folk festivals. Later that year he would join Baez; Peter, Paul and Mary; Odetta; and others in that legendary march with Dr. King.

With Dylan's fourth and fifth recordings, his song content and style shifted again, landing him squarely in the rock arena with the release of *Bringing It All Back Home,* on which "Mr. Tambourine Man" appeared. Dylan's "going electric" created an infamous controversy at the 1965 Newport Folk Festival, the details of which remain in dispute to this day and are certainly moot now.

It is rather remarkable to look back on Dylan's work and achievements and to realize that he didn't win his first individual Grammy Award until 1979. Bob Dylan's entire catalog—from his earliest to his most recent songs—will endure as folk music no matter what arrangement is applied to a given song. It is the lyrical content that has placed all of his works in the context of these modern times, thereby embedding them as the traditional music of the future.

THE VILLAGE SCENE

Just as the songs of Woody Guthrie have become part of the fabric of American song, those of singer-songwriter Tom Paxton have become entrenched in the annals of modern folk history. Among the most prominent voices of his generation, following in the footsteps of Guthrie, Seeger, and others who opened the floodgates to the folk revival, Paxton has gifted the world for more than 40 years with his unabashed tongue-lashing of injustice and inhumanities, his humorously right-on swipes at the "absurdities of modern culture," as he puts it, and his unforgettable songs that warm the hearts of all.

"The Last Thing on My Mind," "Ramblin' Boy," "Bottle of Wine," "The Marvelous Toy," "Goin' to the Zoo," "One Million Lawyers," "Yuppies in the Sky," "Whose Garden Was This?" written for the first Earth Day, "Modern Maturity," and his world anthem "Peace Will Come" are but a few shining examples, classics all. He preserved interest in the music of Mississippi John Hurt by composing his tribute "Did You Hear John Hurt?" to the legendary figure, whose seminal recordings were cut months before the Great Depression, but who reemerged to wow the crowds at the 1964 Newport Folk Festival. Hurt died just two years later, his delightfully syncopated style of folk blues living on in Paxton's song.

Paxton's originals have been covered not only by folk performers, but by artists in arenas from country to pop to opera, including Willie Nelson, Harry Belafonte, Simon and Garfunkel, José Feliciano, Pat Boone, Nana Mouskouri, Bobby Darin, and Placido Domingo. Dolly Parton, in duet with Porter Wagoner, had her first hit single with "The Last Thing On My Mind."

Ever on top of timely topics with what he calls his "short shelf life songs," Tom put his pen to the pedal when he wrote "I'm Changing My Name to Chrysler," about the controversial 1979 federal loan guarantee; in 2008 circumstances called for updating it to "I'm Changing My Name to Fannie Mae." In addition, Paxton's recordings and books for children add to his extensive catalog. The recipient of numerous awards and honors, he received special recognition from The Recording Academy in 2009 with its Lifetime Achievement Award. Read more from Paxton himself in an interview in chapter 9.

Dave Van Ronk was a Village fixture; he lived there from the early 1950s until his death in 2002. It is said that there probably could not have been a folk revival without Van Ronk, "the Mayor of MacDougal Street," as he was nicknamed. Before one even gets to his music, one has to note his generosity and warm heart. He befriended and mentored many a young folk artist, among them Dylan, Tom Paxton, Joni Mitchell, and Christine Lavin. His music ran the gamut of his eclectic taste, from jazz to ballads to blues to Bertolt Brecht. His sense of humor was well known, and in the greater New York City/New Jersey area, at the very least, his "Garden State Stomp" is always fun to hear on radio. The entire song is devoted to listing a plethora of New Jersey's most unusual, most difficult to pronounce place names, nothing more, nothing less, from Allamuchy to Timbuctoo.

During the late 1950s and into the sixties, New York City's Washington Square in Greenwich Village became *the* meeting place for musician and singer jam sessions. Every type of folk music was heard here, from traditional ballad singing and old-time music to bluegrass and a variety of ethnic folk forms. Many who went on to notoriety, if not fame, were an integral part of this folk community.

Musicians Happy and Artie Traum, brothers originally from the Bronx, were part of this active folk scene. The two played music together and separately over the years and with various complements of others, most notably as part of the Woodstock Mountains Revue. Both were among the foremost proponents of fingerstyle guitar. While they primarily played folk, blues, and bluegrass, Artie settled more comfortably into jazz and jazz-infused folk for most of his work during his solo career, cut short when he died in 2008. Happy and his wife Jane founded Homespun Tapes in 1967 to provide expert teaching tools to those wanting to learn how to play. The company continues today as one of the leading sources for instructional materials. Happy also served for a time as editor of *Sing Out!* magazine and appears on several tracks backing Bob Dylan on his *Greatest Hits Volume II* album.

Two especially significant groups that came out of this environment were the Greenbriar Boys and the New Lost City Ramblers. The Greenbriar Boys put a new kind of urban stamp on the traditional sounds of bluegrass, contributing to that genre's expansion and popularity. Its original members, John Herald, Ralph Rinzler, and Bob Yellin, were the writers of "Stewball," recorded most famously by Peter, Paul and Mary.

The New Lost City Ramblers were originally formed in 1958 by Pete Seeger's half-brother Mike, Tom Paley, and John Cohen. Tracy Schwarz, also familiar to Cajun fans, replaced Tom Paley along the way. For 50 years this group was at the forefront of preserving authentic traditional ballads as well as showcasing intricate instrumental ability. Each has also pursued individual endeavors through the years. Mike Seeger alone played an extensive diversity of instruments; he passed away August 7, 2009, within weeks of a farewell—and final—New Lost City Ramblers performance.

Doc Watson was not a New York City musician; he is, rather, from North Carolina. He gained much of his earliest notoriety playing the Gaslight and other Village clubs. Blind from infancy, Doc put flatpicking guitar on the folk map with his lightning-fast playing of old fiddle tunes. He is the "real deal," having been brought up in the music, singing with his family. He would be the first to tell you that as long as it's good music, it doesn't matter what you call a particular style. He is revered among fans of folk, old-time, bluegrass, blues, and rockabilly alike. At age 86, as of this writing, he tours selectively throughout the United States.

LINKS IN THE CHAIN

Joan Baez. Beausoleil. Billy Bragg. The Byrds. Harry Chapin. Tracy Chapman. Leonard Cohen. Judy Collins. Shawn Colvin. John Denver. Ani DiFranco. Donovan. Bob Dylan. Steve Goodman. Nanci Griffith. Woody Guthrie. Tim Hardin. John Hartford. Richie Havens. The Kingston Trio. Lead Belly. Gordon Lightfoot. Kate and Anna McGarrigle. Melanie. Joni Mitchell. Mike Nesmith. Phil Ochs. Odetta. Tom Paxton. Peter, Paul and Mary. Linda Ronstadt. Tom Rush. Buffy Sainte-Marie. John Sebastian. Pete Seeger. Michelle Shocked. Simon and Garfunkel. Bruce Springsteen. James Taylor. Sonny Terry and Brownie McGhee. Richard Thompson. Suzanne Vega. The Weavers.

Some of these names may be familiar to you; others, perhaps not. What do they have in common? All appear as entries in *Folk and Blues: The Encyclopedia*. And they all appear in *The Rolling Stone Encyclopedia of Rock & Roll* (third edition).

Surprising? Not really. *The Rolling Stone Encyclopedia* strove to include those artists who contributed to the building of rock and roll. This demonstrates how intricately interwoven folk is within popular music, and how it continues to be integral to emerging styles. *Time,* in its March 1, 1971, issue (page spread 46–47), depicted "An Informal Genealogy," described in its caption as a "cartoon chart" showing "rock evolution from roots in country, folk and blues." It was a wonderful, if incomplete, snapshot of how no genre is an island; there are many rivers and tributaries. One only has to visit the Rock and Roll Hall of Fame and Museum to grasp the roots/routes that rock has taken since its beginnings in folk music, pushed to the fore by Woody Guthrie.

As the mid-sixties arrived, folk music was still in high gear, but the landscape for music in general was changing. First came the British Invasion—the Beatles, the Rolling Stones, and many more. On the heels of these British exports—who readily acknowledged direct influence from American blues, country, and folk—came a young Scotsman, compared by many to Bob Dylan. But Donovan was his own performer, and quickly overcame any doubts held by audiences on both sides of the Atlantic. His earliest hits, "Catch the Wind" and "Colours," were followed by Buffy Sainte-Marie's "Universal Soldier." He was invited to appear at the Newport Folk Festival in July 1965, the same year of the Dylan uproar.

Mere weeks prior to Newport, a single was released on June 5; it would alter the course of folk music, in effect, creating a new genre—folk-rock. The Byrds recorded Bob Dylan's "Mr. Tambourine Man," with a novel introduction and electric instruments. Roger (Jim) McGuinn, using his Rickenbacker 12-string guitar, kicked it off and shifted the signature to 4/4 time from 2/4. Three weeks later, it was the number-one song in the country. When the Byrds followed up later that year with Dylan's "All I Really Want to Do" and then Pete Seeger's "Turn, Turn, Turn," it sealed the deal on a new approach to folk music, gave the Byrds (and later Roger McGuinn as a solo artist) a signature sound, and effectively changed the course and direction of the folk revival.

On the West Coast in 1965, another groundbreaking group formed. Pioneers of psychedelic rock, the Grateful Dead were known for their improvisational approach to their music, famously incorporating blues, country, and folk in their repertoire. The Byrds went on to a more definitively rock sound, while Donovan followed suit in a more subtle, "soft" folk-rock style. Among the next songs he recorded were "Sunshine Superman," "Mellow Yellow," and "The Hurdy Gurdy Man." Today, still writing and performing, Donovan remains one of the greatest and most influential folk-pop-rock poets to emerge from that era.

The Byrds continued to shift focus as personnel changes occurred. In 1968 they released the seminal *Sweethearts of the Rodeo*, turning to bluegrass and country songs—reverting back, in essence, to a more "folk" sound. Among the tracks were Bob Dylan's "You Ain't Goin' Nowhere," Woody Guthrie's "Pretty Boy Floyd," and the traditional "I Am a Pilgrim."

The year 1967 was known as the "Summer of Love," and as the hippie culture moved into view, folk music came to be associated with "peaceniks" and "flower children." In reality, hippies gravitated just as much, if not more, to rock music as to folk music. Folk music was taking on many flavors, however. Artists such as Simon and Garfunkel were considered folk with their release of "The Sounds of Silence" that year, as were such groups as the Lovin' Spoonful with John Sebastian, the Mamas and the Papas, and the duos Chad and Jeremy and Peter and Gordon, both from England.

And in an ironic twist of events, Arlo Guthrie, Woody's son, released his first commercial recording of the now iconic antiwar anthem "Alice's Restaurant," in November 1967, only a little more than a month after Woody died. The song repaved for posterity the folk road Woody built, and ensured his legacy would be carried on by his son and, ultimately, by other Guthrie family members as well.

Genre distinctions, for the most part, just didn't seem necessary 40 years ago. It became more of an issue when FM radio took hold and radio stations began to cater to specific programming tastes, including the emerging headier rock music with long-play album cuts.

Forty years ago, the Woodstock Music and Arts Fair took place in August 1969. It serves as a great example where genres mixed and blended on one stage over the three days, yet no one seemed to question the diversity of the great music that was presented. Amid rock, soul, and electric and electrifying blues were such folk and country-folk performers as Richie Havens, Joan Baez, John Sebastian, Melanie, Arlo Guthrie, and Crosby, Stills, Nash and Young.

The decade ended; the Beatles parted ways; and it seemed the folk revival was over. I prefer to say, it was only resting and rethinking how to continue to reach a new, younger generation.

NOTES FROM A BLACKLISTED JOURNALIST

I suppose it is not by happenstance that I ended up working professionally in folk music, although I did not consciously set out to do so upon graduation from college. But one might say it is in my genes.

My father, Norm Ledgin, also a journalist-author, was very much the activist for human rights "back in the day" when folk music brought those issues front and center and when this country, in turn, brought many of its artists, including Pete Seeger, before the House Un-American Activities Committee (HUAC). While not called before the HUAC, Norm is listed on page 119 of the U.S. House of Representatives Report No. 378, 82nd Congress, First Session, April 25, 1951, which condemned a Peace Offensive, supported by a few hundred distinguished patriots with whom he is listed as opposing manufacture, storage, and use of nuclear weapons, either by the U.S. or (what was then) U.S.S.R.

While attending Rutgers University, Norm was a reporter and, for a period, editor-in-chief of the school newspaper, *Targum*. As such he was afforded the opportunity to cover a Paul Robeson concert on campus. As it turned out, he was the last journalist to interview Rutgers University's most famous alumnus, Paul Robeson, before Robeson was banished from his alma mater as a result of his political beliefs.

In response to my e-mail query of June 23, 2009, about that interview, Norm recalled, "In January of 1947 neither of us knew he would not be invited back. Robey was a giant, with a booming voice and large physical stature. He was un-hurried in responding to me, a freshman reporter, although due at a post-concert reception. Before parting we stood in the snow and discussed his plan to portray Gideon Jackson in Howard Fast's *Freedom Road*. Years later, Fast told me the movie project fell victim to the Cold War, as did Robey's singing and acting career."

I also asked Norm about his being blacklisted as a result of his beliefs and activist involvement, and how folk music played a role. He related, "The lyr-ics I heard from Josh White and Paul Robeson—the Woody Guthrie and Pete Seeger songs we sang as early as high school—said what was in my heart and mind. They protested injustices like racial segregation, advocated respect for the inherent dignity of people everywhere, and advanced the principles of peace.

"Whether we advocated for peace and social justice by singing, assembling, speaking, or writing, in the late 1940s and early 1950s this wasn't the America the Founders visualized. What better ways for paranoid right-wingers to put down 'troublemakers' than label us outcasts, deny us public access, and ruin our careers? It's important to notice that people like Pete Seeger kept singing anyway, and that our notions of peace and social justice are now more ac-ceptable."

4

No Boundaries:
New Folk to Anti-Folk

In the broader public eye, as folk music became more visible and more embraceable as *folk-rock,* its more traditional forms seemed to gain vibrancy. Almost an underground movement, old-time music experienced a surge of interest and activities in the seventies and through the eighties. Old-time jams, fiddle contests, and festivals became very happening events. Not all, but many of these took place up and down the Appalachians, where authentic players were more accessible.

The oldest, continuously run fiddlers' convention is held annually in Union Grove, North Carolina. Steeped in old-time traditional music, Fiddlers Grove Old Time Fiddlers and Bluegrass Festival was founded in 1924 as a fiddlers' contest, which remains its focal point. In addition to the army of fiddlers dueling it out, the festival offers performances by national and regional artists, storytelling, clog dancing, and workshops, all in a family-friendly atmosphere. Fiddle competitions date to Colonial times, to the 1730s or earlier, making them the true forerunners of modern folk festivals.

Brandywine Mountain Music Convention was a premier Mid-Atlantic area event, first held in 1974 and fueled by the folk revival's impact on interest in preserving tradition. During its two decades in existence, it presented authentic old-time performers mixed with a younger generation of revival musicians. Among the many legends that graced its stage were Ola Belle Reed, Roan Mountain Hilltoppers, Tommy Jarrell, Ramona Jones, Lily Mae Ledford, Wade and Julia Mainer, and Elizabeth "Libba" Cotten.[1]

---

[1]The festival was produced by the all-volunteer Brandywine Friends of Old-Time Music, an organization which still exists and which continues to sponsor regular old-time and bluegrass concerts in the Delaware/New Jersey area, and which puts on the annual Delaware Valley Bluegrass Festival, a mainstay since 1972.

Libba Cotten's discovery is an unusual story. It was a chance misadventure that brought her into the lives and home of the musical Seeger family. Mike and Peggy Seeger are two of the younger half siblings of Pete, born to Charles and his second wife, Ruth Crawford Seeger, an avant-garde composer. Working in a department store, Cotten found a young Peggy lost and returned her to her mother. A grateful Ruth gave Cotten her card, inviting her to call if she ever needed a job. Some time after, she went to work cooking and cleaning for the Seegers.

As a child in North Carolina, Cotten had been surrounded by music, mostly African American spirituals sung from oral tradition. Never learning to read or write music, she taught herself first how to play banjo and later guitar—both upside down because she was left-handed (that is, fretting with the right, picking with her left). She was a quick study, having only to hear a tune once or twice to learn it. However, with her unique picking style—now standard fare in folk-guitar accompaniment—she rarely played a song identically as before.

Surrounded by music in the Seeger home, she was eventually discovered there for her extraordinary, authentic talent. Her signature song is "Freight Train," which she wrote when she was but 11 years old. Libba Cotten recorded her first album in 1958, *Negro Folksongs and Tunes,* and went on to appear throughout the country on many prestigious stages, including the Newport Folk Festival. Most of her recognition came late in life. She was awarded a National Heritage Fellowship in 1984 and a Grammy in the category Best Ethnic or Traditional Folk Recording for *Elizabeth Cotten Live!* Cotten passed away in 1987 at the age of 94 (age disputed).

Mike Seeger, mentioned in the previous chapter, was one of the foremost preservationist-performers of old-time music. Peggy Seeger is best known for her work with Anglo-American folk songs and activist songwriting, particularly with a feminist focus. She will be forever linked with her first life partner, English songwriter Ewan MacColl, whose exquisite love song "First Time Ever I Saw Your Face" was written for Peggy. Most identify it with the 1972 Grammy Award–winning version sung by pop and soul stylist Roberta Flack, whose own music background was steeped in gospel. Flack is but one example of the bridge served by folk music to other genres. Among other definitively folk material she covered in the seventies are Bob Dylan's "Just Like a Woman" and Buffy Sainte-Marie's "Until It's Time for You to Go."

While two original Roan Mountain Hilltoppers, mentioned earlier, have passed on, Bill and Janice Birchfield continue to keep the family group going with additional musicians filling out the band. Playing the music of their Roan Mountain, Tennessee, home, the ensemble has a most unusual performance credit that is pop-culture history. Concept performance artist—and controversial former Sex Pistols manager—Malcolm McLaren tapped the Roan Mountain Hilltoppers for the 1982 "Duck on the Oyster" track for his first album, *Duck Rock,* a seminal work in which McLaren merged hip-hop with Appalachian traditional folk. Another cut on the album—which charted in the United States as well as in the United Kingdom—was "Buffalo Gals," in which a square dance is called over a hip-hop scratch track.

Although old-time music flourished for roughly 20 to 25 years following the folk boom era, it then dipped. In recent years, however, it is making a comeback with a twist. Younger players are adding novel mixes to age-old music, expanding its appeal in the process by making it more palatable to an "under 25" crowd that might not otherwise be exposed to traditional music. By doing so, it is providing the much-needed infusion of youth to keep alive an older art form. The approach some of these innovative performers take to old-time music is not unlike how classical music has preserved and expanded its form and reach for hundreds of years, as new composers opened their ears and minds by incorporating outside influences into their music.

A number of long-established events continue today, with new ones devoted exclusively to old-time music harder to find. Rather, there has been a definitive shift in a large percentage of folk festivals to be more eclectic, opting for terminology that includes, rather than excludes, a particular genre or sub-genre. One hears festivals referring to themselves as "roots music" or "Americana" events, either of which can include old-time artists. The term "folk fest" has also come to mean just about any and all forms of folk music, from contemporary singer-songwriter to old-time music to alternative folk. While bluegrass festivals typically are devoted to that genre, many do include in their lineups old-time groups.

Today, old-time music, pure or blended with inventive sounds, is once again a thriving aspect to the 21st-century folk fabric. Among players continuing the tradition are such artists as Ola Belle's sons David and Ralph Reed, Orpheus Supertones, Cathy Fink and Marcy Marxer, David Holt, Suzy and Eric Thompson, Rafe Stefanini, Stairwell Sisters, Carolina Chocolate Drops, Cathy Barton and Dave Para, Foghorn String Band, Alice Gerrard, Ebony Hillbillies, and Uncle Earl.

A short-lived, specialty spin-off from the group Uncle Earl was formed by clawhammer banjo player Abigail Washburn—who called upon her fluent Chinese faculty. She teamed with five-string banjo virtuoso Béla Fleck, Grammy-nominated fiddler Casey Driessen, and renowned cellist Ben Sollee in the Sparrow Quartet for a limited tour and a 2008 recording. The music merged old-time, bluegrass, jazz, original material, and traditional Chinese folk, crossing global boundaries in the effort.

OLD MEETS NEW

As we entered the seventies, music of all genres was expanding rapidly. It was easy for a niche genre such as folk to get swallowed up and lost in the mix, especially in an era when rock music was exploding and going in many different directions.

Contemporary folk revival practitioners settled in for a long decade in which they continued to ride on the coattails of the initial surge, but with visibility low-key and largely lacking. Rock and roll, quickly growing into its many offshoot genres, was the preferred headline in newspapers and music publications alike.

Precociously seeing the rock writing on the wall, *Rolling Stone* magazine hit the streets in 1967. Yet in its November 9 debut issue, there was folk, front and center: an interview with Donovan. Interesting to note in that issue as well was editor Jann Wenner's review of the brand new Arlo Guthrie release, *Alice's Restaurant,* in which he predicts correctly, "There is something happening here and it is obvious." From that auspicious start, *Rolling Stone* set the pace and standard to not so easily dismiss folk music, but rather to understand its inextricable link to the new rock and roll gripping the nation and the world.

As the folk revival waned, folk music was by no means dead as bemoaned by many and addressed in print in the May 17, 1969, issue of *Rolling Stone* by then *Sing Out!* editor Happy Traum. He pointed out that, while folk had taken a dive in terms of commercial visibility and viability, it was in fact the backbone, the critical catalyst, for the popular music emerging like a locomotive barreling down the tracks full steam. There was no separating rock and rhythm-and-blues music from their Anglo and African American folk roots. Traum went on, rightfully insisting that the "death of folk music" was nothing more than an "illusion," and that the folk boom was "an evolutionary step in an on-going process." He could not have been more right on.

The counterculture had matured into the culture. With its songs of socio-political commentary and antiwar declarations, folk music had mirrored the values and social conscience of the times, turning it toward a heightened awareness in this country, the new, hard-to-ignore electric music better equipped at the time to carry the messages and values that folk music instilled.

Now that we are into the 21st century, folk music is repeating history; it is exploring, expanding its borders, embracing other genres, combining characteristics for modern expression in these ever-changing times. Sounds a bit like what happened to folk as it morphed into folk-rock in the sixties, then co-opted by rock, soul, and beyond as it carried forward into the seventies, no?

This trend started with the late 20th-century upswing in the number of "contemporary singer-songwriter" artists who fell nowhere but into the generic "folk and coffeehouse" category when pursuing a receptive audience. Baby boomers and sixties folkies were busy running kids to and from school, soccer games, and malls; it left little time to go out and hear live music. Others were parked on family room sofas, watching rental videos and cable television. The Internet had not yet chained many to their computers. While not to blame, per se, certainly these factors contributed to a reduction of live folk music interaction, but it eventually opened the door to new, younger performers and fans.

By the late eighties, singer-songwriters were clamoring and jockeying for gigs. To meet the demand, coffeehouse-style venues began popping up—in church social halls, environmental center auditoriums, and bookstores. The era of "new folk" had begun as we entered the 1990s.

To meet the clarion call, an organization was brewing after an initial meeting in 1989 to discuss the possibilities. The North American Folk Music and Dance Alliance—recently renamed Folk Alliance International—was established formally in January 1990. Its purpose from the start was to promote folk music more widely—and thus increase financial viability for its practitioners—by assisting its artists and related business people in learning how to professionalize their activities. An annual business conference, featuring seminars and showcases, has been held since then, attracting an average of 2,000 participants; smaller, regional spinoffs occur at other times during the year.

And while Folk Alliance encompasses both traditional and contemporary folk music, within its first few years the number of "singer-songwriters"—those who did not fall under the aegis of "traditional," "old-time," or "revival" folk—grew exponentially, flooding the land with an enormous number of singer-songwriters who held promise in their hearts of being the next big thing. Folk music was for sure on the rise . . . but it didn't look entirely the same as it had when the folk revival first began to fade in the rearview mirror.

The music of Pete Seeger; Peter, Paul and Mary; and Tom Paxton packed a punch with concise lyrics set to straightforward melodies. The "new folk" artists, in general, relied on more words that often drifted into crossover sounds. Some were heady, almost ethereal, arrangements, often employing expanded instrumental accompaniment far beyond acoustic guitar only. As a result, new folk compositions became more complex, more pop sounding. It was neither Kingston Trio nor Seeger-style "let's get involved and do something" folk. It was "the" new folk.

With his unmistakable voice, rough-hewn and homey, Greg Brown is one of the leading songwriters to gain prominence from the 1980s' focus on singer-songwriters. After a regular stint on *A Prairie Home Companion*, he began to tour nationally. Greg's music can be viewed as a bridge between traditional and new folk. He is equally at home writing ballads and Appalachian-inspired songs ("Rexroth's Daughter," "Lull It By," for example) as he is with his edgier material, straying into bluesy waters on such numbers as "Evening Call" or "Kokomo." His extensive oeuvre of the last 40 years exemplifies the long road he has traveled in folk music, clearly demonstrating respect for tradition while paving the path for younger songwriters.

Suzanne Vega was one of the leading proponents of contemporary folk almost from the moment her 1985 debut album hit the stores. But it was the song "Luka," from her second album, *Solitude Standing,* which propelled her into the spotlight. Written from the perspective of an abused boy, the song placed Vega—and contemporary songwriting—in a new realm. Vega opened doors for other neo-folk women songwriters, most notably Shawn Colvin, Tracy

Chapman, and the Indigo Girls. In the mid-nineties, Vega took part in Lilith Fair, the tours launched by Sarah McLachlan, which celebrate women's voices in pop, rock, and contemporary folk.

Christine Lavin must have been reincarnated from a vaudevillian prototype. She is a multiple award-winning, all-around entertainer who smartly crafts songs with which we all can identify. Mostly with true-life humor, Lavin's songwriting covers everything from "Cold Pizza for Breakfast" (and who can't relate to that?) to "Sensitive New Age Guy" (hey, we know you are out there), co-written with John Gorka, to "Bald Headed Men" (we *definitely* know you are out there) to her lighthearted heart's sigh "Good Thing He Can't Read My Mind." Lavin has wowed audiences with her impeccably right-on lyrics, wit, and baton twirling since gaining recognition in the mid-eighties. Looking back at her first 25 years as a successful folk performer, Lavin recently completed *Cold Pizza for Breakfast: A Mem-wha?* anticipated for a spring 2010 release (http://tellme press.com).

A little more than 20 years ago, singer-songwriter Tracy Chapman released a self-titled album which skyrocketed to number one, captivating a nation in a post-Reagan climate. It was folk music straight out of the Guthrie genre. Chapman's forte has remained in her straightforward, no-nonsense approach to lyrics and melody. *Our Bright Future* is the latest of the Grammy winner's eight studio albums.

Bill Morrissey is a songwriter with a bent for traditional blues and perceptive, expressive story-song telling. His style, something a bit betwixt and between, could be aptly called new folk traditionalist. Making his first recordings in the mid-eighties, his classic *Standing Eight,* released in 1989, secured his standing firmly in the folk community. With his soft-spoken delivery, Morrissey's shy wit often sneaks up on his audiences. Morrissey has mastered the art of pairing an economy of words with understated melody.

Michelle Shocked was discovered in 1986 by the folk world at large—and the commercial recording industry—when someone taped and released without her knowledge or permission *The Texas Campfire Tapes,* her now famous sessions from the Kerrville Folk Festival. By 1988 she was a sensation with her next authorized album, *Short Sharp Shocked.* Her brand of alt-folk/folk-rock has set standards since that time. A leader in the "artist of an independent mind" department, Michelle Shocked is sampled best in concert, and her 2007 CD, *ToHeavenURide,* permits that in this live recording.

Shawn Colvin is yet another success story on the commercial front, also coming of age in folk music at the tail end of the eighties. She was a winner right out of the gate with her 1989 debut, *Steady On,* capturing a 1990 Grammy for Best Contemporary Folk Recording. The 1996 album, *A Few Small Repairs,* proved to be Colvin's breakthrough project. Released as a single from that project, the haunting murder ballad "Sunny Came Home," co-written with producer John Leventhal, took a double 1997 Grammy win in The Recording

Academy's two most important categories, Song and Record of the Year. In 2009 Colvin released *Shawn Colvin Live*.

Following in the famously independent footsteps of Michelle Shocked is another "folk rebel," Ani DiFranco, the self-described "Little Folksinger." While her music is known in circles as wide as folk, rock, and anything "alternative acoustic," she remains best known for bucking the major label system in the early nineties, establishing her own home for her music—and subsequently a label for other independent artists—thereby setting a new standard for folk and independent artists to achieve financial, not just artistic, success. She has released an impressive two dozen or so solo efforts, and a stunning array of collaborations. Her official bootleg concert releases keep her on the cutting edge of business and artistic innovation.

Folkabilly singer-songwriter Nanci Griffith has reached across genre lines for the two-and-a-half decades during which she has been recording and touring. She is known in contemporary folk and country circles, as well as in the pop world. Her distinctively shy voice coupled with dynamic delivery lends itself well to many platforms. An accomplished songwriter, Griffith is equally adept at selecting material from other exceptional sources. Among her best-known songs are Griffith's "Love at the Five and Dime" and "Listen to the Radio," "Once in a Very Blue Moon," by Pat Alger and Eugene Levine, and "From a Distance," which she had a hit with in Ireland, while Bette Midler did the same in the United States on this Julie Gold composition. As of 2009, *The Loving Kind* is Nanci's most recent release and features 13 all-new songs.

John Gorka first entered the spotlight in 1984 as a Kerrville Folk Festival New Folk winner. Within a handful of years, he was considered by many the leading singer-songwriter on the acoustic music scene. Among the nearly two dozen artists who have recorded his songs are Mary Chapin Carpenter, Mary Black, and Maura O'Connell. With attention to detail in his lyrics, Gorka unfolds his stories revealing a rainbow of emotion, delivered in his soulful baritone voice. On *Writing in the Margins,* for example, John offers a compelling read on love, war, and hope for a better world. *So Dark You See*, his fall 2009 CD, revives old classics alongside compelling new originals.

Part folk singer-songwriter, part comedienne, Cheryl Wheeler is an original and a natural. On stage, she takes you right into her living room, bringing to life characters in her songs and humorous stories. She has been recording since the early eighties, but did not receive appropriate recognition until the end of that decade and into the nineties. "Mrs. Pinocci's Guitar" remains a fan favorite among her many legendary pieces. Dan Seals; Peter, Paul and Mary; Kenny Loggins; Garth Brooks; Suzy Bogguss; Melanie; Bette Midler; Maura O'Connell; Sylvia Tyson; Kathy Mattea; and Holly Near represent an impressive list of those who have covered Wheeler's songs.

Emerging from the Boston 1990s' new folk songwriter community, Ellis Paul is among the leading crossover artists today. Veteran songwriter Bill

Morrissey recognized his talent early and produced Paul's first CD, *Say Something,* in 1993. Although he leans toward a decidedly folk-pop sound in his work, Paul demonstrated comprehension and respect for the Woody Guthrie tradition, when he participated some years back in a tribute tour. His songs have been heard on television and in film. His most recent work is *A Summer's Night in Georgia: Live at Eddie's Attic.*

TIES THAT BIND

While the new folk movement was thriving, an "anti-folk" scene was brewing. Largely an underground movement, anti-folk is a marriage of folk and punk rock, which looks to such artists as Woody Guthrie, Joey Ramone, and Dock Boggs for uniquely blended results. It largely, but not patently, rejects pop-infused folk. It appears to have first surfaced in the mid-eighties in the East Village of downtown New York City.

Musician-songwriter Lach is the acknowledged originator of the anti-folk movement, and he is said to have influenced recording artist Beck. Anti-folk communities are also found in other areas of the United States, including California; greater Philadelphia; Ann Arbor, Michigan; and Portland, Oregon. Some of its leading proponents include Roger Manning, Paleface, Adam Green, Cindy Lee Berryhill, Adam Brodsky, and veteran British rocker-political activist Billy Bragg, to name a few. In addition, Michelle Shocked and Ani DiFranco are sometimes referred to as anti-folk. In the early 1990s, Bragg became involved in Woody Guthrie celebrations and in writing new music to Guthrie lyrics, then recorded by Bragg and American alt-country band Wilco.

Beck was initially ensconced in the New York City anti-folk scene. As a teenager, he was smitten by the folk and traditional blues bug, immersing himself in the music. He moved to New York from Los Angeles to make the rounds of the anti-folk clubs, eventually moving on in his music and his career. His innovative approach to music, incorporating seemingly incongruous genres, has been demonstrated by Beck's success, that diverse music forms can coexist and can draw from each other's roots to meet on complementary ground. His 1994 *Mellow Gold* delivered elements of folk, punk, blues, noise, and hip-hop, while a subsequent recording, *One Foot in the Grave,* is a melancholy folk-tinged effort. A later album, *Mutations,* released in 1998, was similar in its folk feel and landed a 1999 Grammy Award for Beck.

In a similar vein as anti-folk is punk rock–enhanced string band music. Most notable in this subgenre is the duo Uncle Monk, comprised of Tommy Ramone and Claudia Tienan, who blend old-time and bluegrass music with a punk edge, perpetuating a hint of the legendary music of the Ramones, for whom Tommy was manager, producer, and drummer.

Stretching the boundaries of folk music has remained a growing trend. Today, there are numerous offshoots of folk, whose names are many and which generally defy definitive description as they continue to evolve. Just as one person's "regular" folk music might not be another's, the same holds true for "alt-folk," "freak-folk," or "psych-folk," all of which designate folk music in forms that digress from that which was more easily identified as folk as we entered the new millennium. Among these sometimes randomly applied labels, the music represents a gamut that ranges from folk merged with rock, punk, blues, or country, for example, to that which has more psychedelic, folk-rock influences (think: Jefferson Airplane or even Donovan as he turned more electric in his late sixties/early seventies work).

In a slightly different, but related arena, is "world folk," more easily identified as either any traditional ethnic folk music found around the world or a border crossing between two or more of them. While already actively and regularly promoted long prior to the founding of the Folk Alliance, world music was given a boost with the additional visibility Folk Alliance, as a formalized organization, afforded musicians of all folk backgrounds. The recent name change to Folk Alliance *International* from just the continental *North American* reflects this growth of folk and world music.

Especially since the early 1990s, world music has exhibited a greater degree of cross-cultural pollination, sharing traditional music from South Africa, Eastern European nations, French-Canadian Cape Breton, the Iberian Peninsula, India, and a virtual world of others. Some artists are long established, while new bands continue to rise out of the roots of many influences. Those who tour the United States are many, just as we export our artists to bring American folk and bluegrass to audiences abroad.

How homegrown American music is perceived outside our country's borders is especially evident with bluegrass, seen by many within the international community as *the* American folk music, because its inception has a clear starting point in this country—albeit with its tangled roots of early country, Scots-Irish fiddle tunes, blues, and gospel. Japan and the Czech Republic have enormous numbers of followers and practitioners of bluegrass.

As mentioned in chapter 3, Bill Clifton was a leading figure in carrying bluegrass and American folk across the pond. In the 1970s, Kentucky's McLain Family Band introduced bluegrass and traditional mountain music to audiences in more than 60 countries during their United States Department of State–sponsored tours. And since 2005, Bob Perilla's Big Hillbilly Bluegrass has visited and performed in such outposts as Armenia, Georgia, Croatia, Dominican Republic, Azerbaijan, Moldova, and Tajikistan, among others.

The international community has reciprocated lavishly. Just before the official end of apartheid, South African singer Sharon Katz formed The Peace Train, the country's first multicultural-multilingual group. Among the plethora of Celtic ensembles that remain popular on both sides of the Atlantic are the Tannahill Weavers and the Chieftains. From Canada, Cape Breton step-dancing fiddle player Natalie MacMaster remains a singular sensation, while the young Québécois trio Genticorum is stretching the traditional sound even more so with its original material and European genre-merging. From Germany, 17 Hippies draws upon countless folk cultures for its renegade acoustic sound that relies upon such instrumentation as accordion, ukulele, clarinet, Indian harmonium, bouzouki, Jew's harp, banjo, cello, fiddle, trumpet, and others—but eschews percussion.

In this country, Duquesne University's Tamburitzans are billed as America's longest-running multicultural song and dance company. The unique group, comprised of full-time students, features music and dance of Eastern Europe and neighboring folk cultures and tours throughout the United States.

Embedded ethnic folk cultures here continue to expand the parameters of their music, to incorporate other non-American music as well as that which is wholly "American folk." Most notably, the Klezmatics, a world-class klezmer music ensemble, was tapped by the Woody Guthrie Foundation to set newly discovered Guthrie lyrics to music for a collection of Chanukah and other Jewish-themed songs. The resulting CD, *Wonder Wheel,* captured a 2006 Grammy. Woody's one-time mother-in-law, Yiddish poet Aliza Greenblatt, had provided much insight and inspiration, while Woody and his family were living in the diverse Coney Island community of Brooklyn, New York.

Klezmer music continues to undergo a spirited revival as it has for the past few decades, attracting new audiences from varied backgrounds. And several young bands are not averse to melding klezmer's traditional sounds with distinctively American ones. Among them, California's Freilachmakers Klezmer String Band performs its mostly original songs in Yiddish, Ladino, and Hebrew, set not only to klezmer melodies but to Appalachian old-time strains and Middle Eastern music as well.

Along similar lines, classically trained violinist and Jewish music innovator Kaila Flexer and multi-instrumentalist Gari Hegedus recently formed Teslim, in which the duo showcases a stunningly vibrant original sound based around old Sephardic and other Mediterranean region melodies. In addition to using violins, the duo presents its unique music playing oud (an early Middle Eastern lute), *saz* (Turkish stringed instrument), and *laouto* (Greek lute).

The next generation of Cajun cool comes to the table from Feufollet. Steeped in its members' Louisiana traditions, the group injects a youthful infusion of originality into their raucous dance numbers, but more than ably settles comfortably within tradition on other numbers.

SONiA, in her renewed incarnation as disappear fear, continues to break down barriers in her explorative, world/folk/pop culture–crossing music. She tours worldwide, singing in English, Arabic, Hebrew, and Spanish, promoting peace and human rights through her music endeavors.

Chicago-based Sones de México Ensemble takes the traditional *son* form of Mexican folk music and adds all-original arrangements. Spiced with experimental forays into classical, rock, and folk, *Esta Tierra Es Tuya (This Land Is Your Land)* is the group's Grammy Award–winning album in which they give the Woody Guthrie title song a *norteño* treatment, singing mostly in Spanish, and pointing out in the liner notes the song's continuing relevance in context to the national debate over immigration.

21ST-CENTURY FOLK

Many labels continue to be applied to artists whose music does not fit neatly into older "packaged" folk forms. It begs the question, must we label it, or should we not simply have a listen and determine for ourselves whether the music appeals to our taste—rather than to a preconceived notion of "folk music"? Among the current crop of musicians and songwriters whose music has garnered widespread attention for the most unusual or adventurous melody, arrangements, or lyrical content are Devendra Banhart and Gogol Bordello. A host of brilliantly creative artists whose work falls at varying points along the folk-rock continuum includes The Decemberists, Feist, Daniel Johnston, Lavender Diamond, Zach Condon as Beirut/Realpeople, and Fleet Foxes.

Among neo-traditionalist folk performers there exists a truly exciting and diverse set of outstanding names to sample: Michael Merenda and Ruth Ungar Merenda (a.k.a. Mike and Ruthy), Crooked Still, The Wailin' Jennys, Avett Brothers, Red Molly, Sylvia Herold and Euphonia, the Maybelles, Mohave featuring Bing Futch, William Elliott Whitmore, and Diana Jones.

In the next chapter, "The Power of Song," you will discover additional singer-songwriters whose work has impacted or is poised to impact future folk generations. Here are a handful more whose music ranges represent a rainbow of influences, from blues to classical to country. Some are well established, others are just breaking onto the scene. All are more than worthy of the folk label and include Elliott Smith, José Gonzáles, Joanna Newsom, Sean Hayes, Jandek, Sarah Lee Guthrie and Johnny Irion, Vienna Teng, and M. Ward.

The number of newcomer singer-songwriters that emerged as we entered the new millennium is astounding. There is both a willingness to experiment with genre bending as there is a desire, a conscious effort by most, to preserve tradition at the same time. This respect for tradition is as vital to the future of folk as is the need to continually update music for younger ears.

Today's folk music has reached a different plane and exists on a different playing field. With the advent of technology that permits it, folk music is once again poised to compete in the commercial world, much as it did successfully 50 years ago. To face that challenge, the key element of today's folk music remains its lyrical content, whether topical sociopolitical issues (war, AIDS, gay rights, hunger, the homeless, etc.) or expressive ballads—but with added contextual color in arrangements, instrumentation, and presentation. Rather than isolating genres for what some think they "should" sound like,

today's most successful folk artists ignore standard confines and are not afraid
to explore and go outside the box.

Try as I might to classify some of the aforementioned portrayers of folk
music, there are some who might disagree with the categorizations. Therefore,
I invite you to listen with an open ear, an open mind, and choose which from
this large bounty of folk music works for you.

5

The Power of Song

What is the first folk song that comes into your mind when you hear the words "folk music"? Is it a song your parents sang to you as a toddler or one sung in nursery school? Did it come from a cartoon show or from sleepaway camp? Perhaps you are an "aging hippie" who thinks of songs by Bob Dylan, Joan Baez, or Peter, Paul and Mary upon hearing the word "folk."

I have to admit, I do not really recall what the first folk song was that I ever heard, but among the folk songs that seem to have been with me forever are "Michael, Row the Boat Ashore," "Skip to My Lou," "Blue Tail Fly," "Oh! Susanna," and, yes, "I've Been Working on the Railroad," that diehard song of toil my mother used to lead us all in singing as we traveled the country in our over-packed station wagon, taking in the sights and sounds of America. "She'll Be Coming 'Round the Mountain" always seemed to be reserved for the final leg of the journey, our destination nearing as we children grew tired and restless.

The power of song—an expression heard a lot lately in connection with folk music's patriarch of song, Pete Seeger. Through song, Pete has enthused, encouraged, soothed, rallied, and even ticked off a few people along the way during his 90 years walking on this land. Toward the end of the biographical documentary, *Pete Seeger: The Power of Song,* Pete says, "Participation. That's what's going to save the human race." The rainbow race—humanity. And through hundreds of songs throughout our lives, we are moved to participate in the various aspects of our lives—social, political, spiritual, or recreational. Pete has often stated that it is more important when he is performing to get the audience singing—to hear them participate—to hear their voices rather than his alone.

Music moves people to speak up, to sing out, and to effect change. The social importance of song is clear in its facilitation and impact of gathering people together in unity of purpose, to participate in advancing change. America was founded on the hope of change—and through our songs we continue to build a better future for all Americans. These songs have come from pens that have cut a wide swath among such modern-day songwriters as Lewis Allan—composer of Billie Holiday's classic "Strange Fruit" which addresses this country's racial bigotry—John Lennon, Buffy Sainte-Marie, Neil Young, Woody Guthrie, John Mellencamp, Pete Seeger, Bruce Springsteen, and Bob Dylan.

Folk songs take into account topics on just about everything and anything. Topical songs of social and political nature certainly top that list in modern folk. Antiwar songs, antigovernment statements, urban blight and plights, country or rural life, union songs and songs to labor by, murder ballads and love ballads or a tragic mix of both, cat songs to presidential songs, and kids songs—animals a popular focus for the really young ones. We can't forget the bawdy songs and parodies. And how could I leave out train songs!?

As discussed in chapter 1, often traditional songs have changed as they have come down to us over the centuries. A fun example is "Froggie Went a-Courtin,'" which, by some accounts, dates to the 1500s as a ballad only or to the 1600s with the addition of a melody. It is said to derive from the mocking courtship song, "Great Lord Frog to Lady Mouse," about Queen Elizabeth I, who famously spurned many a suitor. Versions have been recorded from artists as diverse as Bob Dylan (from *Good As I Been To You*), legendary guitarist Doc Watson (from *The Essential Doc Watson*), and Bruce Springsteen (from *We Shall Overcome: The Seeger Sessions*). The song has also been performed by Kermit the Frog and Miss Mousey on the original *Muppet Show* pilot, "The Muppets Valentine Show," in 1974 as well as in a *Tom and Jerry* cartoon, "Pecos Pest," more than 50 years ago, sung by Tom's Uncle Pecos.

It seems many performers in the late fifties and early sixties were jumping on the folk music bandwagon as the "folk boom" took hold. It appeared to be rather in vogue to include or record a folk song in one's repertoire, even if the performer was pop, country, or early rock and roll. There were two or more different songs titled "The Folk Singer" that emerged during that era as well, one written by Charlie Daniels and another by Merle Kilgore, both compositions recorded by an array of artists, including at least one dyed-in-the-wool folk singer, Burl Ives. Ives and "the man in black," Johnny Cash, recorded the Daniels song, while Glen Campbell and Tommy Roe—for whom it was a pop hit—covered Kilgore's.

Cash took a poke at folksinging groups when he recorded "The One on the Right Is on the Left," written by Nashville songwriter "Cowboy" Jack Clement. This humorous jab at political incompatibilities, included on Cash's 1966 album, *Everybody Loves a Nut,* sailed onto the *Billboard* charts upon its release.

Song stylist/actor Frankie Laine, who covered many genres over his career, recorded famed folk singer-songwriter Terry Gilkyson's "The Cry of the Wild Goose," released in competition to Tennessee Ernie Ford's more country-tinged version. Crossover country legend Eddy Arnold recorded *Folk Song*

Book, a 1964 album, which went to number four on the *Billboard* country album charts. It included such cuts as Bob Dylan's "Blowin' in the Wind," Pete Seeger's "Where Have All the Flowers Gone," Lead Belly's "Cotton Fields," and Kilgore's "The Folk Singer," mentioned above.

"Turn Around," composed by Malvina Reynolds, Harry Belafonte, and Alan Green, was recorded, among others, by crooner Perry Como, as well as by sixties recording duo Dick and Dee Dee, one of several hits for them. Fans of Showtime's *Weeds* will be familiar with Reynolds's best-known song, "Little Boxes," written in 1962 as social commentary on post–World War II suburban sprawl. The theme song for that series, "Little Boxes," sung by Reynolds, was heard on the premier episode, while an eclectic selection of renditions has been featured on subsequent ones. Among the plethora of diverse artists who have covered it on *Weeds* are Randy Newman, Linkin Park, Pete Seeger, Elvis Costello, Laurie Berkner, Persephone's Bees, Ozomatli, Engelbert Humperdinck, Billy Bob Thornton, Donovan, Joan Baez, Aidan Hawken, and the Decemberists. The McGarrigle Sisters, Kate and Anna, delivered it in French.

Speaking of French, probably a first is a folk singer in a first lady role. In the news from time-to-time is President of France Nicolas Sarkozy's folk singer-songwriter wife Carla Bruni. Her material is a broad range of light country blues to songs in the chanson style.

THROUGH THE YEARS

Folk music has embraced—or has been embraced by—some of the most prolific songwriters of our times . . . and continues to be. In the fifties and sixties, there was in-your-face liberal comedy and political songwriter Tom Lehrer, with his dead-on-target humorous songs. One of his most memorable parodies is "Elements," in which he rattles off the list of chemical elements to the patter tune of Gilbert and Sullivan's lively "The Major-General's Song," from *The Pirates of Penzance.*

The multitextured poetic work of Leonard Cohen that began in the mid-sixties continues to infiltrate and influence young songwriters; the range of topics covered in his works is encyclopedic. While he started out as a product of the folk singer-songwriter movement, his reach evolved to encompass country, cabaret jazz, and a style he has called "European blues." Two of his most enduring songs are "Suzanne" and "Bird on a Wire." He returned to the stage in 2008 after a 15-year hiatus from touring. His enduring impact can be heard in a forthcoming project, announced in September 2009, by Beck. Beck has assembled an array of diverse artists that includes Devendra Banhart; Ben, Andrew, and Matt from MGMT; Wolfmother's Andrew; Binki Shapiro of Little Joy; and Brian Lebarton and Bram Inscore from his touring band to record a cover of Cohen's definitive 1967 work, *Songs of Leonard Cohen.*

Phil Ochs, known to many as "the singing journalist," was the embodiment of sixties topical folk songwriting. He released his first album in 1964, and a mere two years later sold out Carnegie Hall in concert solo. Ochs wrote about topics of the era—civil rights, Vietnam, the plight of miners. While most of his songs were political, others were humorous or serious. Sadly, he committed suicide in 1976 at the age of 35, manic depression shadowing him. His prolific songs—including "Changes," "Draft Dodger," "There But for Fortune," "When I'm Gone," "I Ain't Marching Anymore," and "Small Circle of Friends," to name some of his best known—remain an integral component of many artists' repertoires.

Steve Goodman might not be a household name, but one of his songs in particular is recognized throughout the country, and I would venture to guess, most people could sing the chorus. "City of New Orleans" was a hit first for Arlo Guthrie and later for Willie Nelson. From Chicago, Steve got his start at that city's well-known Earl of Old Town folk music club. Country singer David Allen Coe had a hit with his "You Never Even Call Me By My Name," his brilliant, spoof of stereotypical country music lyrics. Other humorous songs included two about his beloved Chicago Cubs, "The Dying Cub Fan's Last Request" and "Go, Cubs, Go." His serious side was poignantly portrayed in a tribute to his dad, "My Old Man." Goodman died at the age of 36 in 1984 after battling leukemia for many years.

Involved with the Old Town School of Folk Music, Goodman had met and mentored counter-country/Americana artist John Prine there. Prine's classic "Paradise" is but one of his many staples that continue to fill both folk and country slots. In 2007 he released *Standard Songs for Average People,* a duo project with legendary bluegrass singer Mac Wiseman. In the same Americana stream of songs are those of the late Townes Van Zandt, whose compositions loved by practitioners in both camps also straddle folk and country genres. Two endearing examples are the delicate "If I Needed You," recorded most notably by country star Don Williams in duet with Emmylou Harris, as well as by legendary folk guitarist Doc Watson, among others, and the lofty ballad "Poncho and Lefty," a number-one hit on the country charts for Willie Nelson and Merle Haggard.

For more than 40 years, singer-songwriter Si Kahn has worked as a civil rights, labor, and community organizer. His extensive catalog of original political songs, along with a wide range of love, humorous, story, and children's songs, has been widely recorded, among them, "Rubber Blubber Whale" and "Aragon Mill." Si is the founder and executive director of Grassroots Leadership, a multiracial team of organizers who help Southern organizations achieve justice and equity through organizing and action. He recently wrote his fifth musical, *Immigrant,* which tells the story of union agitator and songwriter Joe Hill, this country's most famous labor martyr. Internationally acclaimed multi-instrumentalist John McCutcheon stars in the one-man show, planned for the stage prior to the 100th anniversary of Joe Hill's 1915 execution for murder, the result of a controversial and suspect trial.

Also in the labor singer-songwriter pool is Anne Feeney, the granddaughter of a mineworkers' organizer. She has been touring this country and abroad extensively since 1991, although her activism dates back four decades. Her anthem, "Have You Been to Jail for Justice?" has been recorded most notably by Peter, Paul and Mary.

Bob Norman, who passed away in 2008, was a songwriter and folk singer for more than 30 years. The son of renowned symphony orchestra conductor Victor Norman, he also served as an editor of *Sing Out!* magazine in the seventies and later on its Board of Directors. Bob's notebook of material was highly representative of the era in which he came of age in folk music. His compositions embraced diversified musical influences including contemporary folk, blues, country, and classical, coupled with poetic, colorful descriptions of the streets of New York City to the 'burbs of New Jersey. His fourth and final CD, *Time-Takin' Man,* offers a superb read on his talents, with originals that cover such subjects as childhood memories, dreams, Jersey history, the fall of the Twin Towers (witnessed by Bob from a train), and his long battle with cancer. As he described it on his Web site, bobnorman.com, "It's about life."

Veteran songwriter Michael Smith is best known for "The Dutchman," a hit for Steve Goodman. Suzy Bogguss later recorded it on her number-one-selling *Aces* CD. While Michael's songs have been recorded widely in the broad folk and country spectrum, it was his music for Steppenwolf Theater's 1988 production of *The Grapes of Wrath*—which continued on to Broadway and two Tony Awards—that propelled him into the spotlight.

Anne Hills, an acclaimed songwriter in her own right, devoted an entire album, *October Child,* to the songs of Michael Smith. She is one of the foremost interpreters of song, with a voice that lends itself to a range from folk to classical. Her talents have also taken her to the theater stage from time-to-time, as both writer and actress. Perhaps best known for her collaborative projects, Hills has teamed with Smith over the years to tour and record, as she has with others, including Tom Paxton and Bob Gibson. Hills and Smith also joined husband-and-wife duo Steve Gillette and Cindy Mangsen on a recording entitled *Fourtold*.

STORIES AND SONGS

Many folk performers blend storytelling with their song repertoire. Songs, of course, are stories set to music. The art of storytelling is but another aspect of the folk music world, sometimes difficult to segregate, so it is embraced by many performers in one way or another. Folk singers will more often than not introduce a song with a story behind the song; others interject traditional tales into their repertoire, some humorous, others sad and serious.

Steve Gillette and Charles John Quarto's poignant "Song for Gamble," about the late storyteller-guitarist Gamble Rogers, totally captures the essence of this cherished songwriter. Michael Smith penned "Gamble's Guitar," a bio-graphical tribute. A former member of the Serendipity Singers, Gamble died in 1991 while trying to save a person who was drowning. He considered himself a modern-day troubadour, steeped in the oral tradition of storytelling and philo-sophical humor, not unlike that of Will Rogers and Mark Twain. Each year the Gamble Rogers Folk Festival is held in tribute in Elkton, Florida.

Multiple Grammy Award–winner David Holt has been performing—sing-ing, playing, hamboning, storytelling—folk and traditional music for more than 30 years. An innovator within the field, he brought old ballads, stories, and the instruments into a greater public awareness when he hosted the Nash-ville Network's *Fire on the Mountain* series and currently is host of a North Carolina–based traditional arts program, *Folkways.* The natural ease with which he is able to elicit colorful dialogue from his interview subjects about the music and the musicians has placed him in a position that one could best refer to as "guardian" of folk music. He is not just a spellbinding musician proficient on 10 acoustic instruments, but a fascinating storyteller of folk tales, who can spin a yarn for children of all ages. His most recent story-recording is *Hairyman Meets Tailybone,* a collection of tales he gathered from such geographically di-vergent sources as Alaska, the Carolinas, Scotland, and Ireland.

John McCutcheon has been performing and recording for more than 35 years, with almost that number of albums under his belt. He is nothing short of astounding in his expertise playing about a dozen mostly stringed instru-ments; most fans usually associate his name with the hammered dulcimer. Mc-Cutcheon is a master story-and-song writer/teller for kids and adults alike, relating stories of "ordinary people who have done great things," as he points out on his Web site, folkmusic.com. John's repertoire seamlessly blends tradi-tional music with his original, often topical, at other times humorous, material. For choices in CDs, there are live ones, those for children, collaborative efforts, and those with "short shelf-life" titles, which jab at time-sensitive issues or "dated" people, such as former presidents.

Originally from Tennessee, David Massengill is a songwriter, storyteller, and musician, typically accompanying himself on Appalachian (mountain) dulci-mer or guitar. His songs are detailed pictorials based on true life tales, some a little taller than others. As polished as his songs are, they are equally raw when it comes to conveying the imagery. His eight-minute epic ballad "Number One in America," about the struggle for racial equality, spans three decades in a se-ries of vignettes told in the first person. David's most recent CD, *My Home Must Be a Special Place,* breathes new life into his nearly 30-year career.

Storyteller, narrator, and singer Charlotte Blake Alston revives and puts a new spin on traditional and contemporary stories from the African and African American oral and cultural traditions. She often accompanies herself in perfor-mance on such traditional instruments as *djembe, berimbau, nkoning,* mbira, *shekere,* and 21-stringed kora. Charlotte prepared well to relate West African history-telling traditions of Senegal, Mali, Guinea, and Guinea Bissau, as her

teacher was the highly respected Senegalese griot Djimo Kouyate. She has performed at international storytelling festivals, presidential inaugural festivities,
with orchestras, and for a variety of educational PBS programs.

Roger Deitz is known for his acerbic wit as well as for his serious songs.
Among his popular titles are "The Sheep Dip" and "Fifi the Microwave Pup,"
inspired by urban legend. His regular RagTag column in *Sing Out!* magazine
conveys amusing, modern-day folk tales based on real-life happenstances, crafted
to make the reader both laugh and reflect on life. A new recording, *Jersey Toma-
toes,* a collection of his humorous as well as other songs along with more than
50 RagTag pieces, is in the works.

SPOTLIGHT ON ANTJE DUVEKOT

Antje Duvekot first drew attention on the singer-songwriter scene in the
mid-1990s. Her competition wins read like a who's who: John Lennon Songwriting Contest, USA Songwriting Competition, Falcon Ridge New Artist
Showcase, and her first, in 1995, the New Jersey Folk Festival's New Folk
Showcase. Antje's lyrical compositions are astonishingly perceptive, candid,
and profound. Her melodies entice the listener, like trying to catch the brass ring
on a merry-go-round, spinning as excitement builds with each pass at grabbing
the prize. Her captivating voice ties it all together in her coyly naïve manner.
With her 2009 release, *The Near Demise of the High Wire Dancer,* Antje seems
poised for a Grammy Award or two.

GETTING HEARD

Now a part of folk history—with its entire collection archived at the Smithsonian Center for Folklife—*Fast Folk Musical Magazine* was founded in 1982
by Greenwich Village fixture Jack Hardy and published for 15 years. A combination print publication and recording (originally vinyl, later CD), *Fast Folk*
was formed as a cooperative for new singer-songwriters to release their first
recordings. It featured a fascinating selection of fresh voices on the folk scene.
Among those showcased in/on *Fast Folk* whose careers it helped launch were
such future Grammy Award winners as Shawn Colvin, Suzanne Vega, Tracy
Chapman, and Lyle Lovett, in addition to John Gorka, Lucy Kaplansky, Suzy
Bogguss, Christine Lavin, David Massengill, Cliff Eberhardt, and many others.
Although New York City–based, *Fast Folk* went on the road, recording and pro-
ducing issues with songwriters in Philadelphia, Los Angeles, and cities in New
England and Canada. Many concerts and recordings were hosted at home in
the Village by the legendary club, The Bottom Line.

There are now dozens of vehicles for emerging songwriters on the scene
to receive exposure, learning experience, and feedback. These range from
songwriter circles and workshops to weeklong camps to open mics at local
coffeehouses to major songwriting competitions. Perhaps best known of all

songwriter-only venues is Nashville's Bluebird Café. For more than 25 years it has presented the best original country and acoustic music, garnering a world-wide reputation.

Held deep in the heart of Texas hill country, Kerrville Folk Festival was founded in 1972 by Rod Kennedy. It runs for 18 straight days and nights each May into June. Known internationally as a Mecca for singer-songwriters of many styles—traditional and contemporary folk, Americana, bluegrass, blues, jazz, country, and acoustic rock—the festival has showcased more than 1,500 outstanding singer-songwriters since its inception. The event's focus is to promote up-and-coming artists, while simultaneously presenting recognized, seasoned talent on its stages. Among other key songwriting competitions held in conjunction with festivals are those at North Carolina's MerleFest, Boston Folk Festival, and Falcon Ridge Folk Festival in upstate New York.

Performer-songwriter Ed Pettersen, producer of *Song of America* covered in chapter 2, summed up well the critical elements of folk song. He said, "A folk song doesn't need fancy production. It simply needs to connect directly to the people and get out as quickly as possible."

Here are some additional performing songwriters to check out from around the country—legendary to new kids on the block. They represent a diversity of styles, from revival-era folk to genre-bending new folk, and are just the tip of the large iceberg of talent on the scene: Eric Andersen, Catie Curtis, Kris Delmhorst, Caroline Doctorow, Mark Erelli, Steve Key, David Mallett, Anais Mitchell, Dave Potts, Return to the Dream, Lucy Wainwright Roche, Danny Schmidt, Mariee Sioux, Ernest Troost, Corinne West, Loudon Wainwright III.

Songs speak for themselves. The following interviews represent three of folk music's most enduring songwriters, talking about their music and their craft.

JONATHAN EDWARDS: "SUNSHINE," A FOLK SONG IN DISGUISE

It's one of those songs just about everybody seems to know. Oldies and adult contemporary radio programs play it frequently. It has even been used in two or three commercials. "Sunshine"—that happy-sounding, lively song with the distinctive guitar driven lyrics. The song earned a gold record for singer-songwriter Jonathan Edwards when it flew up the *Billboard* charts, peaking at number four the week of January 15, 1972, on the pop-singles chart.

Jonathan has been a major force on the music scene since that time. Interestingly, before genre labels seemed to come into wider usage and tighter confines, he was already there, a folk songwriter taking his music into places and spaces that we now look at as "new folk," where crossing over into pop or country—now often called Americana—has only in recent memory taken hold. He was ahead of his time, long before the folk community recognized it.

His music of the last 40 years has been heard in diverse arenas. Jonathan has collaborated with such country stars as Emmylou Harris and Jimmy Buffett, the progressively bluegrass Seldom Scene, Irish songbird Maura O'Connell, and the equally gifted songwriters Cheryl Wheeler and Christine Lavin. He has scored for films and has starred in a touring company of *Pump Boys and Dinettes*. Jonathan narrated and performed in the travel series *Cruising America's Waterways*, which continues to make the rounds on PBS.

He is one of the most dynamic performers on stage, interspersing his sets with real-life stories, adding to a heartfelt delivery that brings you right into the living room of his songs. His latest recording is *Rollin' Along: Live in Holland*, released in 2009.

I admit that I was still quite the naïve kid, just starting to be baptized into social and political awareness when "Sunshine" became a hit in 1971. It wasn't until years later that I grasped the lyrics and took a harder listen to this alter-anthem for America's "other" voice. Vietnam, former President Nixon, and all the convoluted politics of the era were great motivators for folk song in the late sixties and early seventies. Jonathan and I sat down for a delightful 15-minute chat prior to a performance for Sanctuary Concerts in Chatham, New Jersey, April 8, 2006.

SPL: What were you thinking about, what was on your mind, when you wrote "Sunshine"?

JE: I had just endured the draft selective service system from the ground up. I had just endured that process where you go and subject yourself to military, institutional abuse in the form of a physical for the draft. It was an especially traumatic experience for me. I ended up hurting myself in the physical itself to try and demonstrate to the people involved, that I wasn't willing or able to at-tend their little war in Southeast Asia, that I had far more pressing business. It was a very unpopular stance at the time, very unpopular. Everybody in the bus that came from our little town to Columbus, Ohio, wanted to go over there and kill. They were jumping around the bus, all "macho-d" out, can't wait to go over there, to Vietnam, and start killing people.

Anyway, that's the context from which I started thinking about that whole experience—the experience with Nixon being our Commander-in-Chief, my father being an FBI agent, about the authority figures in general—and it just lit-erally popped out. The song just literally came to me in about as much time as it takes to sing it. I played it for my friend, Joe Dolce, who later went on to write such memorable things as "Shaddup You Face." I showed it to him 'cause he happened to be the first guy I met. He was out in the kitchen. We had bedrooms that were sort of all around this kitchen, in this big house. We had just a won-derful community to write and create music. We were living in a suburb of Bos-ton. I play it for him and he goes, "I like it, but I don't know . . . go back in your room. Go write a different thing for that." But I never did. And there it is. It was 1970.

SPL: What do you think (or know!) drove "Sunshine" to the level of success it enjoyed initially, crescendoing into a gold record in 1971?

JE: Timing, the timing was perfect. The timing was absolutely perfect for that song to come out. A little guy with a little acoustic guitar, you know, singing this happy sounding song, but which actually came from a place of deep anguish and frustration and anger. Very few of the jocks who were playing it at the time picked up on that angst. They were more interested in "Oh, 'Sunshine.' Great theme for the summer."

SPL: Funny you should say it just that way; I remember it very well. I was young and still politically clueless. I, too, viewed it only as this wonderfully cheery song with this very special energy to it. And I think a lot of us who weren't as aware as we perhaps should have been, weren't really cognizant of the fact of what it was all about at that time.

JE: Right. And I loved that about it. I loved that it had that ambiguity of genesis.

SPL: A lot of people forget that "pop" music is "popular" music; "popular" in the sixties and seventies were protest, antiwar songs, and other social issues. Following up on the comment, do you think the vast majority of people who listened to "Sunshine" took it for the meaning that was its original intent?

JE: No, I don't think people got this, the whole issue about authority figures, and all that, even though it's written out in plain English. I don't think that was too large a factor in people's enjoyment of it. I'm just really very blessed and honored that I had a radio hit, *ever,* never mind my first time out of the box!

SPL: "Sunshine" has an extreme exuberance about it, a lot of "oomph" to its appeal. If you had written the same words with a more bluesy melody, say, Dylanesque style, do you think it would have had the same impact and would have enjoyed the same level of success and notoriety?

JE: I don't think so. Successful songwriting to me is when the music and the words happen simultaneously and support each other, and become greater than either one, the sum of the parts. That to me is the best, most vibrant song that I can come up with—when those two things happen together—and it did on "Sunshine." So I can't really imagine it offhand being anything but what it was. It's not a unique melody. That melody is kind of based in folk idiom, as Dave Van Ronk pointed out to me one night after several drinks.

SPL: Would you please relate the story you tell on stage of when you sang "Sunshine" at the historic Washington DC May Day antiwar protest in 1971?

JE: We had a group, whoever they were at the time. I really wanted to say something about the war and about our government and all that stuff, because it was my age group that was being affected, as it is now—the 18- to 24-year-olds are the ones who are paying the price for this idiocy, and their families, of course. I wanted to have a chance. So my manager reluctantly agreed that I would go play this May Day antiwar rally. . . . And so I went, pulled up to the Washington Monument grounds there and asked a cop—U.S. park police not known for their left-leaning tendencies—asked him where the stage was. He looks at me, he looks in the van, and goes (*Jonathan mimics a stereotypical "hip" voice*), "The whole world's a stage." (*Jonathan laughs.*) And we knew we were in the right place.

Anyway, we made it to the stage. We hung around all night waiting to play, and by the time it was our turn, the sun was coming up. It was May 2, and the crowd had not diminished at all. They had spent the night in sleeping bags and tents and newspaper and tarp right in front of the stage, as far as you could see. And the National Guard was there, marching across the field with chain-link fence—I can see it like it was just now—and taking people away to be arrested. And "Sunshine go away today," I mean, the sun was coming up, the Washington Monument, the tear gas, the rose-colored sky—it was right out of central casting. And I kept scrolling the song, finish it, start it over, finish it, start it over. Because I couldn't dream of anything more poignant or appropriate, like I'd written it for that moment.

SPL: What is folk music to you?

JE: Aahhh, well, we're all just folks, aren't we? (*lightheartedly*) Folk music? It's authentic. It comes from a need to express, a need to relate, a need to tell a story, more than a desire, say, to have a hit. It's more intrinsic and it's more visceral than that. It comes from deeper inside, I think folk music does, than the hit factories that we find now in popular music, and always did. Popular music is popular. And folk music, I often joke—my stuff—I don't consider it folk music. I consider it just music. Is James Taylor a folk artist? Can't say that. Is Bonnie Raitt? I don't think so. Woody Guthrie? Maybe. Arlo? I don't know. But no. You think of the people that you consider to be authentic, and is it *folk* music? Folk music sometimes has a bad name, the "f word," as we call it in the business. If you show up with an acoustic guitar, you're instantly labeled as a folk musician, or a folkie. I'm happy to have any label at all (*laughing*), but I kind of reject that because I believe that I am more than that term connotes.

SPL: Years ago, prior to working professionally within folk music, I never thought of you as "folk." You had a hit on the radio; that was my only frame of reference. But then years later, there you were in the folk circles, going back to roots.

JE: It's where we came from. It's blues obviously, and it's gospel. Obviously, it's not jazz. It comes more from a place that's easier to translate, easier to communicate, than jazz or some other forms of self expression. It comes from a need to pass it on, pass on the story.

SPL: What are the most important, as well as the most exciting, aspects of folk music to pass on to the younger set, to our children?

JE: The authenticity, the immediacy, the reality of a guy and a guitar, a woman and a piano, a band and their mandolins and banjos and stuff, confronting a live audience, without any tricks, without any fixing-it-in-the-studio business. Here it is. And if it translates, if you get it, you should go with it and continue it on. If you're a young person starting out (in music), find an audience and love them.

SPL: How does society benefit from folk music, in other words, why does folk music matter?

JE: It's a barometer of our society, our life. It's one of our checks and balances to communicate through music, because it's a universal language—how you feel about what's going on in the world, even if it's just a love song, or a song about the garden; it's all good. And it matters because without it, life would be way different. If we didn't have people thinking about communicating important issues as well as trivial issues through music, life would be way different and not as rich.

STEVE GILLETTE ON THE CREATIVE PROCESS

What do Winnie the Pooh, Jiminy Cricket, Dumbo (the elephant), Linda Ronstadt, Bobby Vinton, Waylon Jennings, and the Kingston Trio have in common? They have all recorded songs composed by singer-songwriter Steve Gillette. Steve has been a fixture on the folk circuit since influential folk duo Ian and Sylvia first recorded his "Darcy Farrow" in 1966. He debuted in his own voice two years later with the eponymous *Steve Gillette*, on which legendary Buffy Sainte-Marie, among others, guests. "Darcy Farrow," co-composed with Tom Campbell, has been covered by more than 100 diverse artists, including John Denver, Tony Rice, Jimmie Dale Gilmore, Nanci Griffith, the Country Gentlemen, as well as Ronstadt and the Kingston Trio.

Gillette teamed with Rex Benson to pen "Bed of Roses," which has been recorded by such performers as Mickey Gilley, Mel Tillis, Chesapeake in duet with Linda Ronstadt, and Kenny Rogers. Tammy Wynette, together with Joe Diffie, tackled Steve's "Glass Houses," also co-written with Benson.

A Little Warmth, a mid-seventies' release produced by Graham Nash (who also appears on the album), offers a Nashville-tinged folk-rock side of Steve's songwriting. It includes the chart single, "Lost the Good Thing We Had," a duet with Jennifer Warnes, co-written by Dave MacKechnie.

With several solo albums under his belt, Steve joined forces in 1989 to record and tour with his wife, Cindy Mangsen, whose compelling voice masterfully interprets traditional ballads, as she accompanies on concertina, banjo, or guitar. Steve's warm baritone and unique finger-picking guitar style (using a flat-pick and two fingers), alongside Cindy, have been components of other collaborative projects along the way. The duo's latest recording is *Being There,* produced, like most of their previous solo and duo albums, on their own label, Compass Rose Music.

Steve wrote the bible on songwriting, *Songwriting and the Creative Process,* and gives workshops throughout the United States on this art. He is also one of the directors of the premier singer-songwriter event in the country, the Kerrville (Texas) Folk Festival.

Steve gave a glimpse into songwriting and folk music in this e-mail interview of October 6, 2008.

SPL: How do you finesse or perfect your songs?

SG: When I have a few days to devote to songwriting, I love to just immerse myself in the imagined landscape of the best result of the intended song. Creative visualization is the term that has been used. Letting the imagination draw from all the musical-emotional moments that I've experienced, and letting it come to me. My expectation is that it will come, probably in disjointed fragments, but I remain hopeful and welcoming, before moving over and letting the editor take over.

Time is the real element. It's hard to compel the creative processes, better to give time to the work, let it take the time it takes. I've said that I have no illusions of being a great genius (just an ordinary one). Mozart may have been able to dash off a masterful piece of music in days, but I'm willing to put in hundreds of hours if needed to do the best work I can. Again, getting away from the process may be part of the process, too, so it's good to take a walk, or just let it rest for a while.

Rewriting is productive as well. I'm sure you've heard it said that good writing is good rewriting. It's hard to bring all the talent and experience you may have to bear at any one time, so it's good to live with a song for awhile and then review it and improve it if you can. It's an open-ended process, and the key is not to force closure on a song that might have more to say to you.

There are songs that I've written to order, usually in collaboration, sometimes in an overnight deadline situation, but it's not the way I like to write. . . . If I only write one more song that I really love, I'll be satisfied—at least until I've lived with that song for awhile and begin to have the inkling of what the next song might be.

SPL: Do you have a dedicated place for working on your songs?

SG: I'm very lucky to have a terrific workspace. We have one bedroom devoted to our home studio. I have a few good microphones. . . . I use Cubase 4 software on a PC, and record all my writing sessions. I have lots of disk storage, and it's not uncommon for me to use a gigabyte or two in a couple of hours.

If things seem to be going well, I'll save lots of it to listen to later. By being able to keep recording, I don't have to stop the process to write anything down, or worry that I might miss some good impulse that I move on from as things unfold. I recommend working that way. I also use MIDI, which I recommend to all my workshop students and anybody who will listen. . . .

I have a small Mackie 1202 mixer that allows me to listen to tracks that I've already recorded, and to layer guitar and vocal parts, which is helpful. Sometimes that harmony part or guitar lead can open up new territory in the song. I like to have some reverb in the mix, just to inspire my vocal performance. The "dry" voice can be uninspiring, so I indulge myself in a lavish wash of echo which would sound strange to anyone listening at that point. It makes the whole process more suggestive and heroic, and sustains my efforts when I might otherwise be irritable and self critical.

SPL: Definition—or nondefinition—aside, what makes a folk song great and what makes for a great folk song?

SG: Folk music is the first music. It's the music that people have created and performed and shared for all the right reasons. . . . Surprisingly, there is wonderful musicianship in even the simplest folk songs, something of primitive genius that has kept them alive. Most modern music—classical and commercial—draws directly from them. I love the quote from Pete Seeger's father, Charles, the eminent musicologist, who said, "There are only two kinds of musicians in the world; those who know they are folk musicians and those who don't." That's not to say that we can't be creating that timeless grail; we do in spite of ourselves. The only time we don't is when we consciously attempt to fashion a salable product, and forget about the wonder. . . .

Cindy says that a person cannot be expected to be able to write folk songs if they haven't sung a lot of them. I agree. Most of the great performers we've met started with a ukulele—that's a great thing to give a six-year-old. I had one, so did she, and Pete Seeger, and Bruce Springsteen. There is something to be said for the early development of soul-hand coordination. I wish music and all the arts were more of a priority in schools. I'm glad when we see that people have taken that on in their communities. . . .

JANIS IAN: SOCIETY'S SONGWRITER

More than 40 years ago, it was a teenage Janis Ian that burst onto the music scene, with a controversial song that catapulted her into a maelstrom and with a debut album that garnered a Grammy nomination. She was only 13 when she played her first gig, at New York City's legendary Village Gate. She captivated the folk and pop crossover world with her stunningly poignant, brutally open "Society's Child," about a thwarted interracial romance. It was the mid-sixties, a pivotal time in the history of all music, not just folk. The song was precociously light-years ahead of its time. It was met by violent controversy from some corners due to its subject matter, while Janis was resented for her success by many in her own community of folk music peers.

By the time she was 18, Janis was already taking a break from the music. Three years later she returned with the release of the stunning *Stars* album in 1973, which also contained her widely recorded "Jesse," as well as the title cut. Her release, *Between the Lines*, featuring "At Seventeen," garnered two wins among five Grammy nominations in 1975. She continued to churn out songs and albums, gathering honors with global audiences for the next several years.

Then in 1983, life led her to a second, longer hiatus that would not see her return to the music business for nine years. She announced her return with the release of *Breaking Silence*, which brought Janis a ninth Grammy nomination.

In 2002, "Society's Child" was inducted into the Grammy Hall of Fame, followed by "At Seventeen" in 2008. That same year she published her autobiography, *Society's Child*. We communicated via e-mail, September 10, 2008, about the craft of songwriting.

SPL: You draw from the deepest wells of your own life's experiences and emotions, as well as from other inspiring moments—such as when you saw the couple on a bus that was the impetus for "Society's Child." What pointers would you give to novice songwriters?

JI: 1. Write. Write. Then write some more.

2. Remember that everything you write doesn't have to be heard.

3. Pay attention to everything.

4. Learn everything.

5. Don't settle.

6. Trust your talent.

7. Your job is to know. Know.

SPL: How do you finesse or perfect your songs?

JI: Huh. I actually never think about that; it's all part of the writing process, and editing as you go. I think that's probably because I've been doing it so long—it was different when I was younger. But again, it goes back to paying attention, and refusing to settle.

SPL: Typically, how long start to finish does it take you to craft/create a song?

JI: Sorry, there's not really any "typically." "Stars" took two hours and a bit. "At Seventeen" took three months. "My Tennessee Hills" chorus sat around for four years before I found the verse.

SPL: Do you have a favorite room, place, or "environment" in which you create songs?

JI: I have a somewhat dedicated writing room. It makes me happy when I have a low couch and a coffee table. But really, it doesn't matter all that much.

SPL: Definition—or nondefinition—aside, what makes a folk song great and what makes for a great folk song?

JI: Oh, I wouldn't dare . . .

SPL: Which folk songwriters do you point to as your heroines/heroes?

JI: Folk *songwriters?* Wow. No heroines/heroes. I think Leonard Cohen's brilliant. Early Dylan still astonishes me. Lennon-McCartney, ditto.

SPL: Who do you think the hottest young folk singer-songwriters are coming up right now?

JI: <grin> Again, I wouldn't dare!

6

Guitars, Harmonicas, and Banjos . . . Oh, My!

John Denver and Neil Young both paid homage to their critical companions, each with his own "This Old Guitar." George Harrison hopefully didn't cry after he wrote and recorded "While My Guitar Gently Weeps." "Doc's Guitar" gives us a taste of just what Doc Watson's guitar can do. Jimmy Buffett explained that "Tonight I Just Need My Guitar." And Justin Hayward's "Blue Guitar" fit in neatly with the orchestral sounds of the Moody Blues. But John Hiatt threw a "Perfectly Good Guitar" down from the top of a flight of stairs. And in "Thunder Road," Bruce Springsteen sings that he "got this guitar" and "learned how to make it talk."

Guitars. The stuff dreams are made of for many. The other half of a folk duo for most singer-songwriters. The guitar remains the best-selling instrument in America, acoustic or electric versions, any genre. The popularity of the *Guitar Hero* music video series is testament.

When folk music is the topic, the acoustic guitar is the first image that comes to mind. One will often find the guitar used as an illustration in articles or calendar listings about folk music. In addition to its popularity as a ladies' instrument in Colonial times, the guitar also partnered with cowboys out on the range, attested to, and romanticized, in the "singing cowboy" films of the 20th century. Blues musicians relied upon acoustic guitars, later often playing steel guitar using a "bottleneck" slide which produces that sweet, soulful, distinctively bluesy sound. Today's blues artists look to acoustic and electric guitars, depending upon which niche of the music they are performing.

Folk players often only strum their nylon-string or their steel-string guitars, playing rhythm chords to complement their singing. Then there are those artists who demonstrate extraordinary technical expertise. These musicians employ two primary techniques, "fingerstyle," whereby strings are individually plucked to pick out the notes as in a melody line, and "flatpicking," in which a flat plectrum, or pick, is used to note the strings up and down, producing a crisper, louder attack.

Fast and fancy flatpicking is an integral part of bluegrass music, advanced in the folk field primarily by Doc Watson, who was mentioned in chapter 3 as one of the folk revival regulars in New York City's Greenwich Village. The method of flatpicking, however, dates back to the early 20th century, when Maybelle Carter, of the Carter Family, developed a striking way of picking her guitar strings, later adapted and evolved as modern flatpicking. Now often just referred to as "Carter style," it is also known as "drop thumb" or "thumb brush," and was first popularized on the Carter Family recording of "Wildwood Flower."

One of the most prominent flatpickers on the folk scene was Clarence White, who, with his brother Roland, was a member of the groundbreaking blue-grass group, the Kentucky Colonels. But Clarence's notoriety came from his association with the Byrds, participating in the folk-rock group's seminal *Sweethearts of the Rodeo* album and then joining that group in 1968. No one played guitar like White, whose lightning-fast speed and unusual syncopation were legendary, but whose life was cut short when he was struck by a car and killed in 1973.

Mason Williams was a comedy writer for the *Smothers Brothers Comedy Hour* in the 1960s. In 1968, Williams took the folk sound of the acoustic guitar and blended it with pop, hitting a home run with "Classical Gas" at number one on the *Cashbox* Top 100 Chart and peaking at number two on the *Billboard* Hot 100 by August of that year. It later picked up three Grammy Awards and legions of new fans for the acoustic guitar.

MOUTH MUSIC

The harmonica, or "mouth harp," has been immortalized in photographs of everyone from Dylan to Donovan to Doc (Watson) for the contraption that musicians wear around their necks in order to multitask on stage—singing while accompanying themselves on guitar and "blowing harp" intermittently. Small and light, the harmonica fits easily in one's pocket to have at the ready for any impromptu jam session. Sonny Terry, mentioned earlier, was among the leading blues players of his day, the mantle carried forward later by Phil Wiggins. Wiggins, in partnership with Piedmont blues player, the late "Bowling Green" John Cephas, demonstrated the successful merging of African and European elements of the music with on-the-mark harmonica and guitar call-and-response interplay, complementary rhythms, and slurred tones produced by stretched guitar strings and "bent" harmonica notes.

Harmonicas have long been used in early childhood education as a learning tool and for later musical training. The harmonica is believed to have derived from an ancient Chinese gourd and reed instrument called the *sheng*. The German company Hohner invented the first modern harmonicas in the middle of the 19th century, although a couple of earlier, more rudimentary, designs existed. Today Hohner remains the leading maker of this fun—and healthy—instrument.

According to several newspaper accounts in the last few years, harmonica therapy is quickly catching on in respiratory-therapy departments across the country, to assist people with chronic obstructive pulmonary disease, asthma, and other bronchial conditions. By a patient's listening to his own breathing, the exhalations and inhalations heard when blowing into a harmonica can be used to learn how to breathe more efficiently.

Harmonica joins a selection of wooden flutes, pipes, recorders, Jew's or jaw harps, and bagpipes, among others, as oft-employed folk instruments. While bagpipes are often the butt of many a joke or cartoon—Heathcliff was spotted on November 23, 2007, handling telemarketing calls by answering the phone with bagpipe music—they are, of course, a most respectable instrument. Used solemnly for funerals as well as in the liveliest of Celtic dance tunes, bagpipes date to ancient times and are found in a wide variety of folk cultures.

One of the more unusual folk finds that you will encounter is "Totem Pole" Rik Palieri, the foremost American folkie player—and perhaps the only—of Polish bagpipes. A multi-instrumentalist and songwriter, Rik related the story of his quest to learn the bagpipes in his insightful book *The Road Is My Mistress: Tales of a Roustabout Songster.*

BANJO. 'NUF SAID?

Banjo was propelled into the folk music spotlight near single-handedly by Pete Seeger. It was his tool to get his music out there, to be heard, to get people singing. Pete's *How to Play the 5-String Banjo,* first published in 1948, remains the bible for folkies worldwide as they tackle the instrument that has come to symbolize protest in folk song. Just as Woody's guitar was emblazoned with "This machine kills fascists," Seeger's banjo carries the message "This machine surrounds hate and forces it to surrender."

Bluegrass pickers, as well, often cite the Seeger manual of instruction as their initiation into the club of banjo picking. Pete updated his book in a later edition to provide detail on the then up-and-coming three-finger style of playing, advanced by Earl Scruggs and known as the signature sound for bluegrass. Among Seeger's students was Eric Weissberg, who years later would become best known for delivering "Dueling Banjos" in the captivating 1972 movie *Deliverance.*

Quite thorough in its coverage of styles, a section is also devoted to old-time frailing, or clawhammer, banjo technique. And for those moments when the banjo in and of itself just isn't loud enough, Pete provides a chapter entitled "Whamming (A Style of Strumming When You Are in a Crowd and Have to Make a Lot of Noise)."

FIDDLING FEVER

In folk music, fiddle is more prominent in the traditional settings of old-time music. However, as folk music continues to expand its breadth and depth, fiddle has become more frequently heard as a side instrument, as has mandolin. The sound of the fiddle brings into the mix elements that can range from a classical orientation to jazz or blues, or ethnic-infused arrangements. Celtic fiddling is among the liveliest and is identified widely with *Riverdance, Lord of the Dance,* and other similar spectaculars. Historically, it has been referred to as the "devil's instrument" or the "devil's box" for just such frenzy it can instigate by its driving, frenetic sound.

Two extraordinary musicians stand out for the interest in and exposure to folk-style fiddle playing they generated. John Hartford was a unique entertainer, who could not be easily tagged because most of what he did was wholly original. John created his own niche simply by virtue of his diverse talents. Fiddle tunes and steamboatin'—he was a licensed riverboat pilot—were his two primary passions. John was known not only for his fiddle playing and great, deadpan stage humor; he was a natural storyteller, a talented multi-instrumentalist, and a gifted songwriter. Many will remember his performances on the *Smothers Brothers Comedy Hour.* His song, "Gentle on My Mind," remains one of the all-time most recorded/most played songs.

Former child-prodigy fiddle champ Mark O'Connor is a name now known on an international scale. His fusing of homegrown fiddle music with classical and jazz has given him a place alongside such earlier contemporary composers as Aaron Copland and Leonard Bernstein.

UKES ALIVE!

A ukulele revolution is afoot. This folk instrument packs a powerful punch among folkies, harkening back to childhood, during which time many of us were first introduced to the pint-sized instrument. Many a folkie cites ukulele roots, among them Joni Mitchell, Cheryl Wheeler, Ruth Ungar Merenda, Steve Gillette, and Cindy Mangsen. Arlo Guthrie secured the uke's place in folk history with his rendition of the Richard Whiting–Gus Kahn penned "Ukulele Lady," included on Guthrie's 1972 *Hobo's Lullaby.* Baby boomers and their parents will remember entertainer Arthur Godfrey, who garnered huge interest in the fifties, playing ukulele on his television and radio shows and giving the occasional on-air lesson as well.

While most people further identify the ukulele with Hawaii, it has its origins in Portugal. Well-known Portuguese luthier Manuel Nunes, whom some call the "inventor of the ukulele," immigrated to Hawaii from Madeira in 1879. He facilitated the transformation of the Portuguese *braguinha* (sometimes known as the *cavaquinho*), a diminutive guitar-like instrument also with four strings, into the Hawaiian ukulele. He was one of the earliest makers of the instrument there. With a handful of design and tuning changes, the ukulele became popular among the Hawaiian native people who gave it its name, which means "jumping flea."

The ukulele has a relatively new star in its corner. Jake Shimabukuro has received worldwide acclaim for his innovative—and extraordinarily speedy—ukulele renditions. Releasing his first CD in 2002, he has encored with several more, including the award-winning 2006 *Gently Weeps*. Jake's repertoire runs the gamut: His virtuosity is an adventure through jazz, blues, funk, classical, bluegrass, folk, flamenco, and rock. He has toured with Béla Fleck and the Flecktones and Jimmy Buffett's Coral Reefer Band, among others.

SWEET DULCIMERS

Another folk favorite for its size, portability, and relative ease to learn is the mountain, or Appalachian, dulcimer. In the absence of guitar, it is often the instrument of choice for solo voice accompaniment, typically in more traditional folk settings. The word dulcimer derives originally from the Latin *dulcis,* "sweet."

Jean Ritchie, discussed in chapter 3, put the mountain dulcimer on the folk map in the fifties. Her dulcimer instruction books are owned by many an aging folkie and continue to be the bible for this instrument. Among younger musicians, David Massengill typically accompanies himself with mountain dulcimer, while musician-educator Phyllis Dunne holds championship titles on the instrument.

The mountain dulcimer has a long sound box, like an elongated violin body, with a fretboard over which three or four strings pass. It is usually played flat on one's lap, or by some professional players, suspended with straps around the neck to facilitate playing while standing. It is fretted with a "noter," often a thin stick of bamboo or similar item, and strummed or struck (and occasionally plucked) preferably with a feather quill, alternatively with a guitar pick.

Similar instruments to the Appalachian dulcimer are played in the folk cultures of Scandinavia and northern Europe, including the *langeleik* in Norway, the *scheitholt* in Germany, the *langspil* in Iceland, and the *humle* in Sweden.

A second type of dulcimer is the trapezoid-shaped hammered dulcimer. Actress-comedienne Whoopi Goldberg famously keeps one in her bathroom (or so she reported many years ago in a television interview). I don't know if that's where I would want mine, but I'll bet the harmonics are out of sight.

The hammered dulcimer is believed to have its origin in either China or Persia (now Iran). This beautiful, full-bodied instrument packs a powerhouse of orchestral-like sound with its many strings, the number of which varies depending upon size of a particular model. It is found in numerous ethnic musics around the world, including that of Greece, Hungary, Switzerland, India, and Germany, among others. Struck with light mallets, or hammers, the "courses" of strings are set up in octaves, piano-like.

Performer Walt Michael is foremost among those who have placed hammered dulcimer music beyond its more customary Appalachian and Celtic settings, lending its sound to other more modern acoustic folk sensibilities. Walt was among many who were influenced by and learned from Bill Spence, who took the hammered dulcimer to new heights in Fennig's All-Star String Band, formed in 1970 and which still performs today. To match Bill's expertise and enhance the dynamics of his playing, the Bill Spence model dulcimer was developed and crafted by Oklahoma-based luthier David Lindsey. Malcolm Dalglish, John McCutcheon, and Mary Faith Rhoads are also part of that elite few whose hammered dulcimer talents are exceptional.

HEAVENLY AUTOHARP

Baby boomers were often introduced to music in elementary school with the strumming of an autoharp. Autoharp was also prominently featured in the sixties by John Sebastian in the folk-rock group Lovin' Spoonful. The beautifully strummed full notes are heard on that group's "Darlin' Be Home Soon," "Day Dream," and "Do You Believe in Magic." "Mother" Maybelle Carter's autoharp playing has been inspirational to many. Reese Witherspoon reproduced the emotive feeling Maybelle coaxed from her autoharp when she portrayed Carter's daughter, June Carter Cash, in *Walk the Line*. Crossover singer Sheryl Crow played an autoharp as she sang at June's funeral in 2003.

The autoharp is among popular folk-accompaniment instruments because of its relative simplicity. The easiest way to describe an autoharp is that it is like a zither or psaltery. Invented in the late 1880s, the autoharp has 36 strings with standard 15 or 21 muting bars, positioned across the strings to form chords when pressed against the strings. Autoharps became a popular folk instrument around the turn of the 20th century.

While a great beginner's instrument, it can also be played with advanced, intricate technique, such as that developed by folk performer Bryan Bowers. Bowers is known for his wide range of solo expeditions on autoharp, ranging from fancy fiddle tunes to elaborate classical pieces. Tom Chapin is another prominent musician who often turns to autoharp for accompaniment; it's a great sing-along instrument and Tom is about as legendary as Pete Seeger for his ability to get everyone singing. Among the many instruments that Mike Seeger played, autoharp was but one with which he carried listeners back in time to authentic traditional music of Appalachia.

BODY LANGUAGE

As diverse as folk music is, the list of instruments is endless. Among others you will hear are accordions, concertinas, and various percussion instruments. What you will not see as often, however, but which will delight and astound you, is a performer demonstrating the not-quite-lost-art of hambone. With origins in West Africa, hambone is said to have been an alternative to drumming for Colonial slaves who were not always permitted to own or use drums. Hambone involves percussive slapping of the chest, arms, thighs, and other body parts, producing tonal differences. Some believe that the term comes from the slang for thigh bone. Others point to the call-and-response lyrics voiced as two people hambone and communicate with each other, which goes "Hambone, hambone, where you been; 'round the world and back again." The hambone here refers to when a hambone was often boiled and reused in soups and stocks over and over until it had been shared by all slaves on a plantation. Mark Schatz, David Holt, and Rodney Sutton are notable hambone practitioners—Schatz currently touring with the Claire Lynch Band, Holt covered in the previous chapter, and Rodney Sutton, a longtime clog dancer who is best known as a member of the groundbreaking troupe, the Green Grass Cloggers.

Footworks Percussive Dance Ensemble, mentioned earlier in chapter 2, is the premier performance group that not only demonstrates hambone, but a wide variety of traditional dance from the Celtic Isles to Appalachia and places in between. Another who carries folk dance across the country is Ira Bernstein, who is a solo percussive dance artist with repeated first-place wins in the Mount Airy Fiddler's Convention Old-Time Flatfooting Competition. He is the director of the Ten Toe Percussion Ensemble, a collective of internationally acclaimed step dance soloists.

Folk dancing remains an integral activity within most folk communities as well as in the larger public arena. Square dancing, contra and traditional country dancing, along with international folk dancing clubs, are found widely and readily throughout the United States.

Odetta, the "voice of the Civil Rights movement," appears at A Folk Celebration, Carnegie Hall, New York City, May 17, 1985.

Tom Paxton sings at the Lincoln Center Out-of-Doors Festival, Damrosch Park, New York City, August 23, 1987.

An example of the diverse ethnic folk found in America are these young Greek-American dancers, entertaining at the Fourth Annual Opa! Big Fat Greek Festival, Flemington, New Jersey, May 3, 2008.

Arlo Guthrie, with daughter Sarah Lee, performs at the Philadelphia Folk Festival, Schwenksville, Pennsylvania, August 25, 2001.

Jean Ritchie sings a traditional ballad a cappella at the Common Ground Roots Music and Arts Festival, Westminster, Maryland, July 8, 2007.

Shawn Colvin guests as a singer with banjo player Akira Satake's eclectic bluegrass band, at the Lone Star Café, New York City, April 10, 1988, a year before winning her first Grammy Award.

"Sunshine" Jonathan Edwards and multigenre artist David Bromberg perform at the Philadelphia Folk Festival, Schwenksville, Pennsylvania, August 27, 1989.

"Zydeco sweetheart" Rosie Ledet headlines the Somerset County Bayou Fest, Bridgewater, New Jersey, August 6, 2006.

In a somewhat rare appearance together, half brothers Mike (left) and Pete Seeger (middle) share the stage, joined by multi-instrumentalist John McCutcheon (right), at the Virginia Festival of the Book concert, Charlottesville, Virginia, March 21, 2001.

Brothers Happy and Artie Traum appear at the legendary Greenwich Village club Gerdes Folk City, New York City, August 7, 1983.

Footworks Percussive Dance Ensemble hoofs it up at the Common Ground Roots Music and Arts Festival, Westminster, Maryland, July 8, 2007.

Janis Ian appears at the Philadelphia
Folk Festival, August 16, 2008.

Multi-instrumentalist-storyteller David Holt entertains at
the Philadelphia Folk Festival, August 17, 2007.

Santa Cruz River Band incorporates traditional American folk into Mexican and indigenous music of the Southwest at the Philadelphia Folk Festival, August 19, 2006.

David Lindsey demonstrates one of his handcrafted hammered dulcimers at the Common Ground Roots Music and Arts Festival, Westminster, Maryland, July 7, 2007.

The rootsy Lovell Sisters entertain at the Philadelphia Folk Festival, August 17, 2007.

Family entertainer Tom Chapin engages the audience in Buccleuch Park, New Brunswick, New Jersey, July 19, 2001.

Youngsters check out some of the instruments for sale at the Common Ground Roots Music and Arts Festival, Westminster, Maryland, July 7, 2007.

Utah Phillips delights the audience
at the Philadelphia Folk Festival,
August 25, 2001.

The Hunterdon Fiddle Club treats patrons to a free concert at the Hunterdon
County Library, Flemington, New Jersey, May 15, 2009.

Piedmont blues stylists "Bowling Green" John Cephas, guitar, and Phil Wiggins, harmonica, join Doc Watson on stage at the Merle Watson Memorial Festival (now Merlefest), Wilkesboro, North Carolina, May 1, 1993.

Native American folk artist Bill Miller appears at the Philadelphia Folk Festival, August 26, 1989.

An ASL interpreter works with Schooner Fare on stage at the Great Hudson River Revival Clearwater Festival, Croton-on-Hudson, New York, June 21, 1986.

Woodstock legend Richie Havens performs at the Lincoln Center Out-of-Doors Festival, Damrosch Park, New York City, August 24, 1986.

Legendary 100-year old bluegrass and old-time musician Wade Mainer and his wife Julia perform at ROMP, the River of Music Party, Owensboro, Kentucky, June 23, 2007.

7

Folk: Family-Friendly

Folk music and family. Perfect together.

In a techno-age where one practically has to stand on one's head to get the attention of kids, folk music could not be a better motivator. It is easy, accessible, and fun. It promotes communication, interaction, and participation on many levels.

Folk music as a family activity goes way back . . . to the definition set forth by those in academia. It is an oral tradition passed down, generation-to-generation, and among one's own community. Therefore, it should come as no surprise that you have read about many folk performers in this book whose parents and other family members were among the first to introduce music into their lives. And just as that is so, contemporary folk performers are continuing that tradition with their children and extended families.

The Guthries are at the head of this class. Not only does Woody's son Arlo carry on the music, but Woody's daughter Nora preserves his legacy through the many activities of the Woody Guthrie Foundation. Arlo's daughter, Sarah Lee Guthrie, is a well-respected singer-songwriter in her own right, performing Americana-branded material as a duo with husband Johnny Irion. Arlo's multi-instrumentalist son Abe is a member of his dad's backup band, while two other daughters, Cathyaliza and Annie, remain largely behind the scenes, maintaining the business aspects of the music. Wife Jackie has been at Arlo's side for the past 40-plus years; she is *the* original cheerleader for this "first family of folk music."

The extended Seeger family, too, continues the tradition, most notably among the younger generation with Pete's grandson, Tao Rodríguez-Seeger, often by Pete's side in performance. Tao was a member, along with Ruth Ungar Merenda, Michael Merenda, Michael's brother Chris, and Jake Silver, in the 21st-century alt-folk group the Mammals, currently on hiatus while members pursue individual musical endeavors. Tao continues to make fused alt-folk/ rock and roll music fronting his own group, while Michael and Ruth now perform as Mike and Ruthy, mentioned in chapter 4. Ruth is the daughter of musician Lyn Hardy and Jay Ungar, the latter the musician-composer of "Ashokan Farewell" mentioned in an earlier chapter.

One cannot talk about family music and folk music in one breath without pointing to Tom Chapin and the extended Chapin family. Son of legendary drummer, the late Jim Chapin, and brother of the late iconic singer-songwriter Harry Chapin, Tom is the quintessential family performer. His music-related activities—songwriting, recording, touring, storytelling—are not just award-winning, but extraordinarily prolific.

Tom began recording with brothers Harry and Steve in the mid-sixties, eventually going solo. In the mid-seventies, he hosted the Emmy and Peabody Award–winning children's show *Make a Wish*. Tom added numerous Broadway and television credits along the way, receiving the coveted Parents' Choice Award for his first children's album, *Family Tree,* which remains a classic. With more than a score of children's books, adult, and family recordings under his belt, Tom remains committed to global hunger and environmental issues, among other humanitarian ones, as he continues to garner awards and kudos.

Chapin's musical energy and productivity appear boundless; in June 2009 he released his 20th CD, *Let the Bad Times Roll,* on which his daughters Lily and Abigail join him. They also perform independently, along with sister Jessica Craven, as the Chapin Sisters. Jazz-tinged, urban folk story-songs is how Jen Chapin describes her musical output. Jen is the daughter of Harry and Sandy Chapin, and it was Sandy who wrote the lyrics to Harry's well-known "Cat's in the Cradle." Steve Chapin continues in his musical endeavors as a multi-instrumentalist composer and arranger, among other pursuits. All come together for Chapin family musical events on a regular basis.

Another folk music family tree includes the complex one of the McGarrigles, Wainwrights, and Roches. Sloan and Loudon Wainwright III (who appeared and sang in a handful of *M.A.S.H.* episodes) are siblings. Anna and Kate McGarrigle are sisters and Kate is the ex-wife of Loudon, whose marriage produced Rufus and Martha Wainwright. Lucy Wainwright Roche is the daughter of Loudon and (another) ex-wife Suzzy Roche. Suzzy performs with her sisters Maggie and Terre, as the Roches. Sloan Wainwright's son is Sam McTavey. All of the above (and I hope I didn't leave anyone out) are folk performers somewhere along the folk continuum. And I would be remiss if I didn't mention that Wainwright patriarch, Loudon, Jr., was the well-known journalist, songwriter, *Life* magazine editor, and author of *The Great American Magazine: An Inside History of Life*.

Other performing offspring include Bethany Yarrow, daughter of Peter of Peter, Paul and Mary; Bob's son Jakob Dylan; Josh White, Jr., whose father was discussed in chapter 3; the late Merle Watson, who was Doc's son and performing partner; and Merle's son Richard, who now tours with his grandfather. In bluegrass circles we find Gary performing with dad Earl Scruggs and Jonathan following in John McEuen's footsteps. John's brother William produced the seminal *Will the Circle Be Unbroken* project in 1972 for the Nitty Gritty Dirt Band, of which John was a founding member.

In bluegrass music and old-time music, family bands are quite prevalent; therefore, the list is endless. One of the hottest bluegrass groups currently touring worldwide is the family Cherryholmes. Del McCoury Band gained great acclaim following the success of *O Brother, Where Art Thou?* and the subsequent *Down from the Mountain* tour. Del's sons Ron and Rob play mandolin and banjo, respectively, in dad's band. And in the genre's tradition of producing precocious young bluegrass pickers, Sierra Hull—featured as an 11-year old rising star in my first book, *Homegrown Music*—still in her teens, is, in 2009, at the top of the charts, fronting her own bluegrass group and about to head off to Berklee College of Music.

The neo-traditional Homegrown String Band bills itself as "the family that plays together." And from Canada, taking their country, ours, and many others by storm are the two teenage Abrams Brothers, whose third teenage member of the band is their cousin. Read more about the Abrams Brothers—fourth-generation musicians—in a special interview in chapter 9.

KID SPEAK

Performing for children takes a special personality and approach. Wife-and-husband duo Kim and Reggie Harris have been conducting special children's programs, along with adult ones, for 30 years. Expanding upon our interview (see chapter 3), Kim mentioned how parents get enthusiastic about folk music as a result of what their children bring back, and also the role music plays in education in general.

> When we go to a school and we do an assembly program, there are times that we'll do a folk concert nearby. And all of a sudden we'll see kids in the audience. The next time they come to the concert, they drag their parents there. . . . If kids get excited about the music, these days parents are (then) excited about something that kids are really into, and that's positive. . . .
>
> . . . There's also an emphasis in using the arts as a part of teaching . . . educators realizing that not only music, but the arts are an effective tool for teaching and can help them . . . to teach content. . . .

Husband-and-wife John Kirk and Trish Miller head up the group Quickstep. They have long been on the leading edge of educational entertainment groups, with their repertoire of fiddle tunes and traditional and original songs. Trish is a former member of the legendary Green Grass Cloggers and plays banjo, guitar, and ukulele. John is a multi-instrumentalist who also dances and whose song, "Long Roads," was recorded by the Dixie Chicks. John and Trish take their exciting family programs of music and dance to schools, libraries, and festival workshops.

In the Midwest, many a school and library program has been treated to the music of Phyllis Dunne, the 1985 Woody Guthrie Folk Singing Champion and a multiple award-winning Appalachian dulcimer musician. An accomplished pianist as well, Phyllis often teaches and performs with husband Bob, who mesmerizes audiences with his masterful playing of the Aboriginal wind instrument, the didgeridoo, traditionally made from eucalyptus trees hollowed by termites.

Internationally acclaimed Canadian entertainer Raffi is probably the best-known children's troubadour. His recordings, books, and videos have fed folk and acoustic music to two generations over the past 30-plus years. His classic songs "Baby Beluga" and "All I Really Need," among countless others, provide positive musical messages to pass down to future generations. *Songs of Our World* celebrated our planet and the human family as Raffi served up more than a dozen tracks in a variety of languages.

KIDS FOR KIDS

When kids see and hear other kids playing guitar and singing songs or playing fancy fiddle tunes, it interests them and they can relate because it's someone their own age. Since 1994 the Saline Fiddlers have been inspiring other high schoolers to pick up a fiddle and bow and let 'er rip. The extracurricular music program was initiated to offer an alternative style of music education to public school students in Saline, Michigan. The Saline Fiddlers have carried music, song, and dance from the traditions of American folk, bluegrass, jazz, Western swing, and Celtic music to audiences throughout the United States. It is estimated that there are now at least 1,000 similar fiddle groups around the country.

By chance, I stumbled across one in my own backyard. The Hunterdon Fiddle Club was founded in 2005 at Hunterdon Central Regional High School in Flemington, New Jersey. Comprised of about 30 students from the school's orchestra program, virtually all came into the Fiddle Club with a background only in classical music training, yet, like the Saline Fiddlers, this spirited ensemble has embraced a diversity of styles, including folk, bluegrass, Irish, blues, and Hungarian czardas. A side project of the school's orchestra, the Hunterdon Fiddle Club presents holiday and spring concerts and makes other area appearances. Such exposure to folk music, when joined with a curriculum of classical, offers unlimited opportunities for youngsters to understand and connect the roots of all music, not just the roots of our own American music.

AND FOR THE BIG KIDS . . .

A limited number of colleges now offer specialized programs and degrees tailored to Appalachian studies or bluegrass music. Community colleges and folklore centers, too, often host short-term courses, such as "Music of the

Catskills and the Hudson River Valley," recently taught by veteran performer Bob Lusk in upstate New York.

One year-round traditional music and arts program is Common Ground on the Hill. Its focus is on diversity being a unifying force. In addition to a wide range of music, dance, and art programs, Common Ground hosts an annual nonviolence institute to address social interaction issues that challenge our modern society. Weeklong summer sessions include youth-focused programs, as does its annual Music and Arts Festival.

Sponsored by various local folk organizations, folk music weekends are scattered around the United States. These unique events offer age-specific activities, so that families are able and encouraged to bring their children. Such weekends typically comprise concerts, square or contra dances, workshops such as banjo or guitar, and sing-alongs. Summer months find a host of intensive, weeklong music camps, many of which cater to children's learning possibilities. Summer also brings hundreds of folk and bluegrass festivals throughout the country. Workshops for kids and adults are often integrated into the programming schedule.

The appendix, "More Folk: Selected Resources," offers additional information on instructional materials, learning camps, and more.

DAVE FRY: RATED G

Dave Fry is a renaissance man in the folk world at large. He formed his first folk band nearly 40 years ago while in college. By 1976 he had founded one of the most important venues on the folk music circuit that continues to attract national and international artists. The 100-seat Godfrey Daniels, located in Bethlehem, Pennsylvania, remains popular with fans that will often drive across two state lines to attend concerts. Through his affiliation with the Touchstone Theater company in the 1980s, Dave developed presentations for children, which since then have been the hallmark of his work. Mixing in bluegrass and good old rock and roll, Dave takes kids of all ages along for a folk music ride that is always fun as well as educational. Dave and I spoke on Earth Day, April 21, 2007, after his set at Deer Path Park, Readington Township, New Jersey.

SPL: What makes performing for children so important to you?

DF: I get a lot back, for one thing, because they react more and it makes it a very immediate experience for me, which is what I love. But also it's a challenge. And folk music is not just for them. It's not just singing along, it's dancing. The dance part comes right away. You see little kids up dancing before anything. If you look at folk music, folk music has always been a communal event, where people get together. They dance, they sing, they do things together. And when that happens, community happens. I know if you look back pre-electronics, that's why you had square dances, that's why you had church sings, and people getting together and singing because the community was so important. For kids, it's the same thing. That's how they get to dance with each other, how to use their bodies, how to use their minds and their voices, in a very unpressured situation.

I recently did a project in Bethlehem, Pennsylvania, called PASELA, integrating arts and literacy for preschool kids, pre-K and kindergarten. It was a real eye-opener. They would sing along and they would want to get up and dance immediately. And since I was in the classroom all day, I noticed that a lot of stuff bubbled up later, especially when their hands were occupied with maybe eating or something, where stuff that I wasn't sure that they got, until two hours later when all of a sudden, it starts to bubble up in their conversation and they start singing at the dinner tables. So that was one very eye-opening experience.

And then I did a 10-week period for two-year olds which changed my way of thinking completely. What was interesting with that is they're so tactile. I'd take my banjo in and they would just come right up and put their hands on my banjo. And I basically couldn't get through a song. So I was fairly desperate and then I realized, well, you know they just need to synthesize the rhythm in their hands. So I got egg shakers and maracas, fairly adult-friendly sounds (*laughing*). Very important, that's why the little shakers are so nice. And they don't hit people and they can't swallow them (*laughing again*). Pretty basic stuff. But in that way, we can get through a whole song, and then you could also work with different rhythms, speeding up, being able to dance and shake at the same time, and express to the fullest extent through their voices and their bodies as people should do (*laughing*). Somehow we all forget how to do that. So that's the immediacy of that stuff that is really striking.

SPL: Why are folk music and kids a perfect match?

DF: Because they don't have any preconceptions about it and society hasn't gotten to them yet. They are very much open to using their voices and singing and experiencing the music to the greatest extent. And folk music is not something that you witness and that you watch on television or you necessarily listen to, at least for me. It's something that you experience, you do it yourself. You jump in and be part of it. It's not a third person type of thing. And the kids realize that. It does present problems with control, but that's where the craft is—learning how to control the experience, so that it doesn't become chaotic.

SPL: Is folk music a tough sell for parents who might not, shall we say, already be folk enthusiasts?

DF: Well, you know, when I do the family things, I pick on the dads, you know, "Come on, sing along," because that's the role model, if dad gets up and sings. My dad sang all the time and my mom played piano. So that really affected me, and it was no big deal for me to do it. But once again, we're kind of handcuffed by society, the arts in general (with the thinking that) folk music in particular is something that you go to a concert for an experience, as opposed to doing it yourself.

When I do my assemblies, I start off with "Yankee Doodle." It's a song they know, and I tell them it's an old song, it actually predates our country, and that it was at one time written by the British making fun of the early colonists. What appears to be a kid's song actually has elements that if you dig under the surface a little bit more, there's politics. That's the thing about folk music. I love it because it exposes culture; you just have to dig a little bit. So they learn a little bit that folk music, that there's a little more to it. And people have been doing it a long time.

I also ask, "What's a folk song?" and they'll say, "Country music." And then I say, well, "Which country?" And they go, "Wow, yeah, you know, Russia has folk music. Africa has folk music. Israel has folk music, everybody has folk music." So it's not what they hear as typecast as country music. So then I do "The Cat Came Back," and that's a little bit more contemporary and just a killer song. And I start to introduce the fact that you can write some of your own words, the folk process of creating, making it an immediate to your own thing. There's one thing in "The Cat Came Back," (the line) "thought he was a goner." One little kid came up to me and she thought (the line was) "lawyer," and I thought that's great, so I sing that version all the time.

Rock and roll is part of my folk music. I grew up listening to the Beatles and all that stuff. So I try to tell them, once again, rock and roll songs where you get up and dance and you sing—that is a folk experience, especially in our culture now. If I do "My Girl," everybody knows it and they almost start doing the dance routine (the choreography). Once again it's relating the dance and the singing and the movement.

But then what I do is, I say, "You kids have your own folk music," and that's when I present things like some of the street corner stuff and playground stuff that they do and that they write and change. And I'm doing some stuff that I've learned from my daughter, and they're great, they're killer, and you don't have to play an instrument to do them. She's now 17 and playing Joni Mitchell on the guitar. She had her ear to the ground. What's fun about them is they are easily remembered and they are great theatrical pieces as well. When you get the kids up and being physical and being silly and everything like that, it's theatrical. And the parents love to see it. And if you can get the parents up to do it and be kind of silly with them, then you've broken through. Then you've knit a small community in that family, and that's what's important.

8

Folk Alive!
Front Porches to Festivals

A sea of tie-dye greets you on a dusty, sticky July day as you pull up to join hundreds of other vehicles parked in a vast farm field, nary a tree in sight, barren—except for the cars, SUVs, and campers ganged up in small enclaves, tents pitched precariously among them. Grabbing your folding chair, straw hat, sunscreen, and water bottle, you hike to the entrance and find that, no, you are not back in the sixties, you are at . . . a folk festival!

Each year, from coast-to-coast, border-to-border—as well as in our Alaskan and Hawaiian outposts—hundreds of folk festivals, concerts, and other related music events of every size, shape, and flavor take place. From daylong small-town street fairs, which feature local folk artists, to citywide affairs that shut down and close off roadways, turning them into temporary malls to accommodate thousands of attendees, folk music has taken this country by quiet storm. While any given event might be well publicized, folk music is often more like a best-kept secret, a treasure waiting to be discovered.

And now that you are armed to discover folk music, where to from here? Let me offer a few starting points around the country.

"Folk Music Capital of the World" proclaims the banner welcoming visitors to Mountain View, Arkansas, home of the Ozark Folk Center.

True or not, for sure an abundance of folk and traditional music is at its core. A village dedicated to providing living history, the Ozark Folk Center preserves, documents, displays, and interprets the cultural and social history of the Ozark Mountain region, an area that includes parts of Arkansas, Missouri, Kansas, Illinois, and Oklahoma. The center offers live traditional music, pioneer crafts from broom making to building a banjo, herb gardening, and more. Visitors are encouraged to participate as well as observe and enjoy.

Before you leave Arkansas, put Eureka Springs on your itinerary. It is the home of one of the oldest continuously run folk festivals in the country, the

Ozark Folk Festival. Held each fall in the city's historic auditorium—whose first performance upon completion in the early 20th century was by John Philip Sousa and his 67-piece band—the event features a cross-section of singer-songwriters and tradition-based performers.

Head east and you can journey The Crooked Road, Virginia's Heritage Music Trail. First envisioned in 2003, the idea was intended "to generate tourism and economic development in the Appalachian region of Southwestern Virginia by focusing on the region's unique musical heritage." Today, road markers identify a 250-mile route through 10 counties, pointing the way to such historical places as the Carter Family Fold in Hiltons, museums including the Blue Ridge Institute and Museum, performance spaces, and exhibits relevant to the rich history of American music in that long alley.

The National Folk Festival, first held in 1934, is a traveling festival produced by the National Council for the Traditional Arts (NCTA) in partnership with communities around the country; as of 2009 it has been presented in 27 cities. Butte, Montana, is the host city for the 2010 event—free to the public. The festival's artistic diversity is matched only by its variety of ethnic and regional food vendors.

The NCTA is the oldest folk arts association in the United States, founded in 1933. It is a private, not-for-profit corporation "dedicated to the presentation and documentation of folk and traditional arts in the United States." Its programs, which celebrate and honor arts that are deeply rooted cultural expressions—music, crafts, stories, and dance passed down through time by families, communities and tribal, ethnic, and occupational groups—include festivals, national and international tours, concerts, radio and television programs, films, and recordings, among others.

The NCTA's "concept" tours have been highly acclaimed nationwide for 30 years. Among the best known have been the Irish-American Green Fields of America and the multigenre Masters of the Folk Violin, in which a teenage Alison Krauss—now a superstar—received much of her early national exposure. In addition, the NCTA has established several regional partner festivals, all of which are also free, annual events. These are the Lowell (Massachusetts) Folk Festival, the American Folk Festival held on the Bangor, Maine, waterfront, and the Richmond (Virginia) Folk Festival, which takes place each fall in its historic downtown riverfront district.

Another granddaddy of traditional folk festivals featuring authentic artists and crafts—and also free—is the Smithsonian Folklife Festival, initiated in 1967. Held on the National Mall in Washington DC, the event draws an average of more than one million people over its two-week-long run each year, always overlapping with the Fourth of July holiday. It serves as an educational presentation of contemporary living cultural traditions, bringing in musicians, artists, craftspeople, storytellers, cooks, and others who demonstrate their creative skills, knowledge, and talents that comprise their community-based traditions.

The seminal Newport Folk Festival celebrated 50 years in 2009, still leading the folk revival, 21st-century style. Returning to its stages for its half-century mark were such legendary figures as Pete Seeger, Joan Baez, and Judy Collins who were joined by relative newcomers including Fleet Foxes and the Decemberists. The Clearwater Festival, begun by Seeger to help promote awareness to clean up the Hudson River in New York, continues each June and is the oldest and largest environmental celebration in the country. Officially called the Great Hudson River Revival, it has won acclaim for its exceptional attention to people with disabilities. Main stage and other areas provide American Sign Language (ASL) interpretation of performances, along with other accommodations for people with disabilities. With an activist area, an extensive craft market, and family-friendly activities, it remains a winner on all fronts.

Two university-based events with several decades under their belts are the Kent State Folk Festival in Ohio, sponsored by that university's public radio station, WKSU, and the University of Chicago Folk Festival, presented by its Folklore Society. Both take place during the academic calendar year and provide a balanced program of folk and roots music, including blues, bluegrass, and old-time. Dozens of traditional and modern blues fests dot the map across the Mississippi Delta region, while the annual New Orleans Jazz and Heritage Festival spans two long weekends the end of April into May. It presents a stunning array of internationally known musicians from just about every genre, including Dixieland jazz, Cajun, zydeco, bluegrass, gospel, blues, folk, and world music.

Hawaii offers a diversified range of native celebrations throughout its islands, as well as numerous year-round showcases of Hawaiian slack key guitar. For those who opt not to hula, there is an active contra dance community. Hawaii's large Celtic community has a plethora of activities to choose from, while the bluegrass contingent is smaller but intense. Juneau is the host city of the weeklong Alaska Folk Festival, now in its fourth decade of offering world-class artists and hands-on workshops to fill a long, cold winter's spell.

Award-winning Falcon Ridge Folk Festival, nestled at the foot of the Berkshire Mountains in New York State, has quickly become *the* place to hear rising singer-songwriters. With a nod to tradition as well, the festival also caters to dancers and families, while hearing-impaired attendees are assisted by on-stage American Sign Language interpreters. The festival site accommodates wheelchairs virtually everywhere, including stage areas, port-a-johns, and at ATM machines, and it hires people with disabilities, staff and performers both. The festival even occasionally hosts a workshop during the festival about ASL and other accessible events.

Also in upstate New York, Old Songs Festival of Traditional Music and Dance, held each June for the past three decades, typically showcases an eclectic lineup of internationally recognized musicians and regional ones, offering the best in American traditional folk, Celtic, and other multicultural genres. Family activities and workshops, such as shape-note singing, are always a part of this highly respected, well-run event.

Heading to the Southwest, the Albuquerque Folk Festival and Tucson Folk Festival are but two splendid places to check out fantastic lineups of folk performers. Participation is key in Albuquerque, where a buffet of hands-on activities awaits festival-goers. Learn to dance everything from squares to Scottish country dancing, or how to play anything from banjo to bouzouki. There are jam sessions, musical petting zoos for the kids (that is, instruments young children are encouraged to touch!), and stage concerts that encompass everything from traditional ethnic folk to contemporary singer-songwriter.

Another free event is Tucson's annual weekend. Tucson Folk Festival's roundup of music, dance, and workshops each May presents 100 local, regional, and national acts that perform a diversity of folk, blues, bluegrass, world music, and more. Four stages are scattered about the downtown area, all within walking distance of each other.

If you are more of a picker, among the top-flight choices is the Walnut Valley Festival in Winfield, Kansas, known as "picker's paradise" and nearing its 40-year mark. The newer Merlefest, held each spring in Wilkesboro, North Carolina, and which honors the memory of Doc Watson's son Merle, has quickly become a mecca for pickers and fans of all styles of acoustic music. Hardly Strictly Bluegrass, a free event located in Golden State Park in San Francisco, is what its name implies; it has an eclectic lineup that ranges from rap to, well, bluegrass.

About an hour from Denver in Lyons, Colorado, the annual Folks Festival will tantalize with its avant-garde new folk artists as well as its established performers and scads of workshops. To exemplify this range, in 2009 the "old guard" was represented by Don McLean (of "American Pie" fame) and the latest in young trendsetters by M. Ward.

Approaching its 50-year anniversary (anticipated in 2011), the Philadelphia Folk Festival laid much of the groundwork for revival-era folk festivals, as it evolved out of the same climate for folk music as did Newport Folk Festival. Each August it presents several stages of music, dance, workshops, and kids-oriented programming, along with a juried craft market and other vendors. On August 16, 2008, I spoke with Festival Chairman David Baskin about how to keep festivals fresh to attract newcomers to the folk scene.

There's a foundation that supports classical music. . . . And they underwrite a lot of stuff. Their thesis is in support of contemporary classical music because all music was new at one time. And I think that's what I've looked at now for the festival. When we started in '62, I mean, who knew Tom Paxton? He was new. Almeda Riddle wasn't, but who knew Almeda Riddle, except for a small group of trad people who followed the traditional music?

You had the traditional crowd and then you had the new crowd, which was who we think of today as the traditional people—but they're not. I mean, there's Tom Paxton, the late Phil Ochs, Tom Rush, Janis Ian, and Judy Collins, and all the people we grew up with who've been around now for 40-plus years, but they were new. So what's next? Do you just keep playing the same stuff over and over again? How many people are going to listen to that who are our age?

I've been doing this since '62 and I'm in my mid-sixties. So what do you do? What do you play for the 18- and 20-year-olds or the 13-year-olds or my grandson who's 7? What's he going to listen to? Yeah, you can listen to Pete (Seeger) and you can listen to Oscar (Brand) and all the stuff that's out there, but hopefully some of the new stuff that's going on—whether it's Devendra Banhart or Espers or Kimya Dawson—and what they're doing is as folkie, I guess, as anything else. I think we have to do that. We as a festival have to keep doing that.

. . . We need to be part of the scene. We're very open here at the festival. We try to be. I mean, look, we don't book Barry Manilow, but guess what? He's a singer-songwriter. Why isn't he a (folk) singer-songwriter? Why is he any less than Ani DiFranco? Dvořák wandered the countryside picking up folk tunes and incorporated it in his *New World* symphony, and Beethoven and Bach and everybody else. Then you listen to Leonard Bernstein or Copland, (they) ripped the stuff off from Bach and everybody else. . . . These are all new things that fit folk parameters? I don't know. I hate labels, so what can I tell you?

Folk festivals, of course, are not strictly American; scores of American folk artists travel abroad each year to perform at music clubs and international festivals around the globe, just as folk artists from other countries perform here in the United States. Our Canadian neighbors have long produced some of the best folk festivals to be found, including Winnipeg Folk Festival, Vancouver Folk Festival, and Mariposa Folk Festival, to touch upon a few.

Across the Atlantic, Tønder Festival is an acclaimed multigenre event in Denmark. Its performers and fans travel from dozens of countries on several continents. Israel's Jacob's Ladder Folk Festival began modestly in 1978, started by young folk enthusiasts who had relocated from Britain and America. Today, it attracts artists from all over and features folk, bluegrass, Irish, blues, and a diversity of ethnic folk. Cambridge Folk Festival in the United Kingdom is a premier event known for its broadly defined folk lineup; it has been a force on the international scene since its founding in the mid-sixties. Resources in the appendix will help you on your way to locate others.

FOLK FOR ALL

As mentioned earlier, there are folk festivals and events, increasing in numbers, that now ensure people with disabilities can also attend and enjoy. The Americans with Disabilities Act set parameters for all entities across the United States to follow and which the folk community at large has led the pack in meeting the guidelines. While I have only mentioned a couple of specific events in this regard, it should be noted that many, if not most, provide at least minimum required accessibility.

While some might think it odd to have music interpreted by an American Sign Language facilitator for the hearing-impaired, it is not surprising or unusual at folk music events. Music is not just melody, it is words. Rhythmic vibrations emitted from instruments are another conduit via which the hearing-impaired perceive and enjoy music. To watch an ASL interpreter work along-side a performer can be rather awe-inspiring. Interpretative expression can be quite creative and fluid—and just as musical as the sounds others can hear.

Pete Seeger and Paul Dubois Jacobs wrote a storybook called *The Deaf Musicians,* which addresses the subject for young readers. And as most will know, Beethoven was deaf and composed some of the world's greatest works. World-class solo percussionist Dame Evelyn Glennie has taken her instruments—which also includes the great Highland bagpipes—to new heights in spite of her in-ability to hear. She recently began teaching privately, which also has allowed her to explore the world of sound therapy as a means of communication (See http://www.evelyn.co.uk.).

More and more is being learned and reported in the media about using music to communicate and interact with children who have autism and other developmental disabilities. Musician John Foley, who has often worked along-side the venerable Oscar Brand, is a music therapist who, with his group Radar Rangers, is among those who reach out and touch with music these special children. In the novel *The Devil Wears Prada* by Lauren Weisberger, reference is made to breaking through with a troubled student after a guitarist is brought into school to sing folk songs.[1]

A ROOM WITH A VIEW

Most of us don't have an Ozark Folk Center nearby, but we do have front porches and backyards. Just as in Colonial times, pioneer days, and the early 20th century, before radio and recordings became common, it was the home place, the town square that played host to music, a family and community affair very much embedded in social and recreational life. Today, we plug into iPods and sometimes forget that music is a very real, human interaction that beckons to be shared with others, not just via direct line into one's ears.

Welcome to my living room. As you enter, you'll notice about 30 people seated on the sofa, on folding chairs, and in various comfy spots on the floor. In front of the bay window is tonight's special guest, who will provide an intimate evening of music for those gathered here. Seated up there tuning his guitar might be Mike Agranoff, a New Jersey entertainer who "sometimes sings folk songs," or it might be the legendary songwriter-singer Janis Ian, or perhaps Tom Chapin, in which case you might see a lot of youngsters sitting restlessly on the floor alongside parents.

A concept not so new, but gaining in popularity, is the house concert. These living room performances are a back-to-tradition, new wave of opportunities

---

[1]For more information about music therapy, contact American Music Therapy Association, http://musictherapy.org.

for many of today's touring artists. They provide a special up-close and personal experience for listener and performer alike. It takes some of the club pressures off the entertainer to be able to sit back and just pick and sing among folks who are like old friends—and many are, for such is how open and comfortable folk music is. It encourages interaction not only among audiences by such activities as sing-alongs or dances, but it would be quite rare for even some of the biggest names in folk not to mingle, chat, and sign CDs for fans. House concerts provide a warm and fuzzy atmosphere, a special sense of fellowship that encourages participation, the root of folk music.

However, it should be mentioned that there has been a movement afoot to keep those putting on house concerts out of trouble with local towns and zoning boards. It can be a fine line between operating a business and hosting a house concert. The vast majority of house concerts put on by folkies, however, do not do so to earn anything beyond the cost of refreshments, typically turning over all fees, or "donations," paid by guests directly to the performer. Most also maintain an e-mail list whereby these concerts are by invitation only or through very limited publicity avenues targeting a specific audience of "in the know" fans. See "More Folk: Selected Resources" for further information on how to find house concerts in your area.

Speaking of Mike Agranoff, besides being a familiar face on the festival circuit as a performer, he is an integral part of an all-volunteer crew that puts on the weekly Minstrel Concerts in Morristown, New Jersey. He shared some time and words with me backstage at the Philadelphia Folk Festival, August 16, 2008. A hint of Mike's quick wit and wry outlook on folk music can be seen in his response to my first interview question, "What does folk music mean to you?" He quipped, "You got a couple of days?" And he went on to provide a long perspective on the academic "authentic" confines, followed by the folk revival era definition, and how the general public subsequently embraced all of it as "folk." He concluded with, "If it takes more than one trip from the car to bring in equipment (for a gig), it ain't folk." Spoken like a true traditionalist.

Agranoff cites David Buskin (not to be confused with David Baskin, above!) as the first folk performer to grab his attention, when Mike attended a show in the sixties at Folk City in Greenwich Village. As Mike described his getting into folk music, "I sort of only got into it really after the Crosby-Stills-Mitchell-Garfunkel era, and backed into it from there. The stuff that was on the FM radio at the time. And then I backed into the more traditional stuff from there."

Mike went on to relate a story that demonstrates superbly the camaraderie typically found among folk performers, well known or locally known. This same approachability and accessibility holds true between fans and top artists. Mike offered this vignette: "In the late eighties, there was a folk festival in New Jersey called the Waterloo festival. They booked a lot of the big acts from the sixties and seventies for the evening concerts, but during the day they had a lot of locals for some of the little things. So I had backstage access and I'm sitting (there) practicing concertina. Arlo Guthrie walks up to me and goes, 'I've always been interested in the concertina. Do you think you could show me how it's played?' So I go, 'Sure, Mr. Guthrie.' So for 10 minutes, I give Arlo Guthrie a concertina lesson."

OTHER SPACES AND PLACES

In addition to house concerts and festivals, naturally there are many other spaces and places to experience folk music. Coffeehouse-style venues still abound, often in rented church halls or community centers. Bookstores, while at one time more active in hosting live music, seem to have slowed in this area, but some do still have the occasional folk artist. Renovated or restored old theaters that seat 200 to 300 are also popular folk music venues, especially because natural acoustics are often ideal and enhance the experience. Major venues, clubs, and 1,000-seat theaters appear to be once again opening up their doors and stages to more folk and folk-related artists.

And cruise ships are opening their decks and ballrooms to folk and roots music. The relatively new "Cayamo, a Journey through Song" cruise has featured such names as Emmylou Harris, Vienna Teng, and Lyle Lovett, among others. For bluegrass lovers, there have been many choices of cruises over the years and these continue to grow.

While some performance spaces are wholly for-profit businesses, most folk music concerts and festivals are still run by an army of faithful folkie volunteers, under the aegis of a local folk organization or association. In addition to concerts, you will find a splendid potpourri of bluegrass, old-time, or Irish jam sessions, as well as "open mics" for singer-songwriters. Folk clubs often host sing-alongs and other similar get-togethers, as well as various dance opportunities, including square and contra dancing and international folk dancing.

To hook into your local folk scene, turn to the resources in the back of this book for starters, and, of course, do an Internet search for your city or town just using the words "folk music," and for sure, many hits will be returned. So break out your uke or banjo, grab the kids, and head out for some great folk music!

9

Bridging Folk: Tom Paxton to the Abrams Brothers

Among the interviews I conducted for *Discovering Folk Music,* I found these two, juxtaposed "old guard versus new guard," splendidly representative to take folk music well into the 21st century, if not beyond. Both expressed sentiments of import to the existence and continuation of folk music, bringing the relevance of folk music into a contemporary realm, while embracing its past.

Tom Paxton, discussed in chapter 3, has already secured a place in the folk music history books. He remains an influential songwriter and delightful performer.

Just as there has been huge impact on American folk music from artists (and songs themselves) from across the pond, many successful folk artists in America over the last 50 or more years have been our close Canadian cousins, among them Oscar Brand, Ian and Sylvia, Gordon Lightfoot, Leonard Cohen, Ferron, the McGarrigle Sisters, and Joni Mitchell, to name but a few. Arriving recently is a group of "under 21" musicians, all from one family, actually from a long family tradition of music.

The Abrams Brothers, John and James, along with cousin Elijah (18, 15, and 18, respectively, at the time of this interview), first stormed onto the bluegrass and gospel scene barely a decade ago. With the release in 2008 of their third recording, *Blue on Brown,* they not only demonstrated precocious musical talent and a keen, innate sense of stage presence but also a deep understanding of the folk tradition. Paying homage to Bob Dylan, Woody Guthrie, and Arlo Guthrie, they have expanded upon their own sound, taking it outside the stricter bluegrass parameters, and have presented the Dylan and Guthrie material in a refreshing, 21st-century forum, easily grasped and embraced by the "under 21" set. More of a "roots-rock" approach—let's call it folk music performed revved up on mostly bluegrass and acoustic instruments—the Abrams Brothers deliver a powerhouse of music from which new traditions can build while preserving its origins. In concert, these young men are captivating and charming; with mastery that belies their youth. Their music and performance style poises them to become major crossover players on stages where genre-labeling is both irrelevant, if not unnecessary.

That the Abrams Brothers have attained veteran status at such a young age is astounding. Their extraordinary talent captured for them the 2006 Daniel Pearl Memorial violin, presented annually to gifted young musicians in honor of international journalist and musician Daniel Pearl, a *Wall Street Journal* reporter taken hostage and killed in Pakistan in 2002. The award is made with the purpose of sharing with audiences Pearl's mission of uniting people through words and music.[1] The Abrams Brothers are exemplary.

RAMBLIN' WITH TOM PAXTON

Interview conducted January 13, 2007, at the Sellersville Theater, Sellersville, Pennsylvania.

SPL: Usually we hear discussion revolving around the "what is folk music" question. I prefer to ask, what is *not* folk music?

TP: I think, basically, what is not folk music is music that is written for the commercial entertainment industry, some of it absolutely brilliant. This is not meant to be a qualitative thing, but I think that a song that is written for Top 40 radio, only once in a million times will it make it into the oral tradition and people will learn it and pass it on. I think folk music mostly is very simple music made by people who are not trained musicians and who have learned a song from someone else.

SPL: Why does folk music matter?

TP: It matters because it really does reflect real life. Even like the goofy fairy tale songs from Elizabethan England and stuff like that reflected the psychology of that era. It made the transfer to Appalachia because people liked to hear the stories, the good stories, full of mayhem and liars and murderers and all that good stuff.

SPL: What is the key to a great folk song?

TP: The key to a great folk song is the same as a key to a great commercial song. And that is, it's a terrific marriage of words and music. A song like "Tom Dooley" jumps into my mind. There really was a Tom Dula. And the song is simple. Anyone can sing the song the second time it's played or halfway through the first time. It's the simplicity of it. There's nothing false about it; there's nothing contrived. That's what catches people, I think.

[1]http://danielpearl.org.

SPL: What three artists, who have appeared on the scene since the year 2000 or thereabouts, do you feel, will have left the most indelible legacies in folk music by the end of this century?

TP: Wow! I don't *know* any folk artists who have really made a mark since 2000. Most of us have been around for a long time. I mean there are "kids" like John Gorka; but he's not a kid any more (*laughing*)! Who would you say?

SPL: I've seen a lot of up and comers. But I'm looking for someone you would like to point to, let's say of the ilk of Ani DiFranco, but, of course, like Gorka, she's been around already a bit longer, too.

TP: I can't name anybody! Shame on me. Oh, I can think of one, Modern Man. Modern Man. Do you know them at all? I think they're hysterical and very, very musical. Now there's not a lot traditional about them, but I just think they're wonderful, so put them down![2]

SPL: How do we ensure that our children's children and so forth hand down, share, and preserve folk music?

TP: I don't think we can. I think each generation makes its own choices. When we've performed and recorded the music to the best of our ability, it's out of our hands. Someone once said something that made great sense to me. He said, "I'm responsible for the effort, not the result. And if we do our best, that's all we can do."

SPL: What is your favorite folk song and what is the very first folk song, or any song, that you recall from childhood?

TP: The first one I recall is "Blue Tail Fly," sung by Burl Ives. But my favorite folk song is probably "Shenandoah." It's such a great song, because it's a very mysterious song. From verse to verse, it doesn't make any sense, which is proof that the one we hear now was cobbled together from different versions. One version of the song as we all know it goes, "Oh, Shenandoah, I long to see you." And then there's that verse that goes, "Oh, Shenandoah, I love your daughter. For her I cross the rolling water." Well, who is Shenandoah? Is she a chick? Is she the chick's father? It doesn't matter; it doesn't matter in the slightest.[3]

SPL: What song would you choose to represent folk music for someone, let's say, who wakes up on an island and says, "Folk music? What's that?"

[2]Modern Man, while relatively recent on the folk scene as a trio, is comprised of three very seasoned performers, David Buskin, Rob Carlson, and George Wurzbach, each acclaimed in his own right. So on the horizon since 2000, not really; will sustain the test of time? Stay tuned . . .

[3]"Shenandoah" is performed widely across many genres, from folk to opera. Opera singer Thomas Hampson gave his exquisite rendition on ABC TV's *Good Morning America,* January 19, 2006, and is found on his 2009 CD *Wondrous Free: Song of America II.*

TP: Hmmm (*pensively*). "Where Have All the Flowers Gone."

SPL: Do you think that a folk music revival, the likes of which occurred 50 years ago, will be seen again, and if so, what will precipitate it?

TP: No, I don't think so (*emphatically*). I think that a constellation of circumstances was responsible for the other one. There was the bubbling of the left wing, of the old lefties from the thirties and forties, and the blacklist. (For) a lot of these people, folk music was an extension of their political philosophy. Then a lot of us came along who loved the music without necessarily loving the philosophy that they espoused. As a matter of fact, by then a lot of them had given that philosophy up as well. But that kind of got it going.

Then the intrinsic beauty of the music—and the incredible breadth of the music—was something that people could get their teeth into. It was a challenge to learn these songs, to play these songs, and learn the guitar or the banjo. That there was a lot to accomplish for an individual sitting alone in a dorm room or something that with some motivation could really get into it.

Then in the sixties, we had one national emergency after another. And they certainly required music. And the music that they required was music that people could make quickly and simply and sing it. Those things don't seem to be applied right now.

We have this God-awful war in Iraq, but we don't have the draft. Our armed forces are stretched to the absolute limit right now. If we go having little pranks with Iran, or something like that, they're going to have to reinstate the draft, and the country will go berserk. So barring that, I don't see the circumstances being the same and I don't see any hint of it, really, in young music.

Another thing that helped us a lot was that the popular music of the late fifties and early sixties was uniquely vapid. It was all this Dick Clark promotion jazz. They'd find someone who looked cute and manufacture a star. The songs were just absurd. So all of a sudden, here came the Kingston Trio and it was a breath of real fresh air. Until the Beatles, folk music had a real run at popular status. Some of us never quite got to popular status in the first place. It was fairly brief as musical moments go, I'd say five years of good. But it did a lot of good. A lot of people got turned on to folk music by listening to the Kingston Trio, and then pursued it and wound up (at) Sleepy John Estes. I think that's one of the great things about it.

SPL: This is very interesting and takes us full circle back to the "what is folk music" question.

TP: I have a great memory of one of my jillion visits to the Kerrville Folk Festival. For awhile there, they called me "the rainmaker," because inevitably, long about my second or third song, it'd *rumble rumble rumble* in the background and, sure enough, here would come up a gulley washer. And it happened on this occasion. So all they do is just stop the show, everyone goes backstage undercover, and wait it out, because it doesn't last long. So there I was sitting back stage with a lot of the younger musicians you know today. And they started singing, "Under the Boardwalk." And I was singing along with them . . . *under the boardwalk*. I love that song! Is that a folk song? Not yet. Not yet. It's known by a whole generation. Will it make the jump? That's the question. But it sure was fun! It sure is a good song! (*Sings "under the board-walk, board WALK." Laughs heartily.*) Great! Good luck writing the book! I know what a pain in the butt that is . . .

THE ABRAMS BROTHERS: MAKING OLD MUSIC NEW AGAIN

Interview conducted with John Abrams via e-mail, December 15, 2008.

SPL: You chose to include the well-known "City of New Orleans" on *Blue on Brown*. Explain the connection you feel to this particular song.

JA: Steve Goodman wrote the song "City of New Orleans." To me, this is a pivotal example of a timeless folk song that can have a lasting effect on multiple generations. This is the type of song that can captivate audiences in multiple genres, as it is not manufactured or marketed to fit a specific criteria or demographic. Due to the strong presence of American history and culture, it can relate to audiences in any shape or form. Not only did Goodman record it, but, of course, Arlo Guthrie, Willie Nelson, and Johnny Cash, to name a few.

SPL: You come from a musical family stretching back a number of generations. How does folk music connect those dots for you in the music you listen to and/ or perform?

JA: Gospel and roots music are very ingrained in the Abrams family. The Abrams Brothers are the fourth generation playing and singing gospel music for audiences across North America. Music to me, particularly folk music, can be considered a language that everyone can understand. We speak it to each other, and the language is passed through the generations mainly by auditory means. So naturally, folk, roots, and gospel music were passed down to my brother and me through our family. We would go over to our grandparents' place for what was then the Abrams Family and Clarendon Station band practices. We would pick up on the Canadian fiddling tradition, bluegrass songs, and the family harmonies by listening. Quickly, we became a part of that tradition.

SPL: What is the first folk song you can recall from your childhood?

JA: I believe the first folk song James and I learned was "The Big Rock Candy Mountains," sung by Harry McClintock.[4] We got into folk and bluegrass when

O Brother, Where Art Thou? hit the screens, and the highly acclaimed sound-track made its way to stores across the world. We were 9 and 11 at the time. James is younger, born March 23, 1993; I was born August 23, 1990.

SPL: If you could speak directly to other young teens, in addition to simply playing them your music, what would you say to them to pique their interest in folk music?

JA: I would ask them if they wanted to listen to authentic music that is deeply ingrained in our history. I really think that teens and children of this genera-tion are searching for music that is real and not manufactured. So much con-temporary pop music has regressed to become a disposable marketing tool to get people to buy product. The Abrams Brothers want to offer this generation a style of music that is compatible with what they are familiar with today (in con-temporary music), yet one that keeps a strong presence of bluegrass, roots, and gospel. Therefore, *Blue on Brown* is more of a roots-rock album, as it combines the two worlds. Not too far away from what the Band, the Byrds, and the Dillards were doing (in the sixties).

SPL: If you could choose only one song to represent the essence of folk mu-sic, what would that be?

JA: Woody Guthrie's "Oklahoma Hills" or Bob Dylan's "The Times They Are a-Changin.'" The first because Guthrie so beautifully describes his homeland, and it is that very presence of family, home, and the things closest to you that form the foundation of American folk music. And the second because Dylan talks about the ever-changing face of our social, cultural, and historical situa-tion. Folk music to me is also an ever-changing art form that continually de-scribes these factors in their many stages. Thus, this song became an anthem in the folk world.

SPL: What is folk music to you?

JA: Folk music is a language. It is spoken between people, and people com-municate with each other through this music. To me, music is a universal lan-guage that everyone can understand. Whether you can play an instrument or not doesn't matter. Therefore, I would say that music, especially folk music, is a far more accurate language describing human emotion, feelings, and soul. For example, (the word) "love" in English often loses meaning, but if love is conveyed in the chord progression of a Leonard Cohen or Bob Dylan ballad, to me the replication of the feeling of love seems more real.

---

[4]Also known as "Big Rock Candy Mountain," it is usually ascribed to McClintock as composer, with authorship having been disputed over the years. His version is heard in *O Brother,* but most baby boomers probably associate the song with that recorded by Burl Ives in 1949, reviving its popularity.

10

A Living Tradition:
The Times They Keep A-Changin'

Folk music in the 21st century has moved far beyond "Kumbaya," yet its legacy remains with us, its future in our trust. Now that we have explored many of the aspects of American folk music, have we, in fact, formulated a finite definition? Or have we determined that it is not possible, let alone entirely necessary, to do so?

Folk music is not static. It is a living tradition. It is handed down and around by oral and aural methods, both traditional as well as technologically advanced. As a result, folk music—American or otherwise—is shared around the country and across continents.

We are conservators of authentic folk music, but in our efforts to preserve it, we also open the door to changing it—not unlike the way ballads first entered this country, then traveled the Appalachians and beyond, lyrics and story lines often altered in the process. Yet they are considered "traditional folk"—by academic standards—and they are still with us. Arguably, nothing was lost in the folk process.

Let's look at some of the characteristics and qualities that we recognize in folk music—in centuries-old traditional tunes and ballads, in spirited revivalist compositions, and in contemporary works whose arrangements are enhanced by multi-influenced infusions that cross cultures as well as genres, yet which still embrace timely topics that affect society.

POETIC PASSION TO SOMBER SOLILOQUY

Folk music serves as both a personal and communal voice. It gives spirit—or solace—to our souls, conscience to our hearts and minds, and stirs passion in our beliefs. Folk music provides a viable pathway to participating in the human race, to paraphrase Pete Seeger. It is a most powerful voice at that—and the earliest voice of humanity, the root of all music.

We use folk music to express ourselves. We can use folk music to reach out to our neighbors next door—or across oceans. Today, folk music in America continues to reflect the melting pot that we as a nation represent. One cannot separate folk music from the fabric with which America itself has come together from its inception. Every immigrant to these United States brought a history and culture from another land. We all share these common threads, roots that intertwine and meet vividly in the music we identify as folk—be it American, Bulgarian, African, Japanese, or Russian folk music. Our diversity unites us, just as American folk music does; it has been born out of many traditions.

And folk music reflects tradition as equally as it does change. It expresses values as often as it speaks from or to the heart. Folk music can teach history as well as lay foundations for the future.

An example of how folk music played a role in building a future was seen during the Great Depression, when folk music was used as a public service announcement. During the Depression, President Franklin D. Roosevelt's New Deal implemented the Works Progress Administration (WPA), through which it put to work several million people over the course of eight years. The WPA built roads and airports, funded the startup of public school lunch programs, and put to work people in the arts—actors, artists, and musicians, among them, Woody Guthrie.

One of the best-known of the more than two dozen songs Guthrie wrote—and was paid for—while visiting dams under construction in Washington State was "Roll On, Columbia." Guthrie was hired by the Bonneville Power Administration to write folk songs that would elicit greater public support of the new government-run hydroelectric dams along the Columbia River, strongly opposed by local private utilities.

STATE OF THE ARTS

In recent years, concern has been raised about the state of the arts in our educational system. Sadly, the United States stands out in the democratic world for its lack of strong and consistent governmental support of the arts; federal funding cuts typically aim first at the arts. Attitudes on the part of decision-makers seem to embrace an ideology that the arts are recreational, as opposed to the reality that they are cultural curators of our rich and diversified heritage.

Simultaneously, music is becoming more segregated into a greater number of labeled styles, more musical niches, which tear apart the common roots. More accurately, perhaps it is the music business itself that permits this or even encourages this further fragmentation. In his *New York Times* op-ed piece "The Segmented Society," David Brooks addressed this issue, citing a new initiative by musician Steven Van Zandt, guitarist for Bruce Springsteen's E Street Band.[1]

In 2007, Van Zandt established the Rock and Roll Forever Foundation. Its purpose is to provide a groundbreaking arts-driven curriculum for middle and high school students to keep them engaged and in school. Music, as Van Zandt notes on the foundation's Web site, is among those things that changed his life and yet, music and arts programs are among the first cuts when it comes to trimming budgets. By teaching the roots of rock and roll, and placing music appropriately within other coursework (social studies, language arts, music, and more), Van Zandt seeks to put relevance into the lives of students who might not feel or find it otherwise.

And while the program is not complete and has not been implemented as of this writing, visit http://rockandrollforever.org, and you will see up front, on the home page, everything *Discovering Folk Music* embraces. Pictured there, surrounding sixties-era civil rights protest signs, are Woody Guthrie, Dr. Martin Luther King, Jr., Joan Baez, Bob Dylan, and Chuck Berry.

Michael Jackson's sudden passing brings up this related point. While he was known as the "king of pop," do people really stop to think about what "type" of music he made—other than great music? There was an early clip revived during the coverage surrounding his death. It exemplified well the deep roots of the rhythms and inflections that showed up in his later music. There was 10-year old Michael belting out—absolutely nailing as if he had lived the life— the blues ballad "Who's Lovin' You," written by Smokey Robinson. Seeing that piece and then hearing sound bites on various stations how his mother had so influenced Michael by giving him "the love of God and country music," there it was—gospel, country, and blues—all folk music with a lot of soul at the heart of Jackson's music.

GUARDIANS OF FOLK MUSIC

There is folk in all of us. Therefore, it is our responsibility to keep folk music alive, no matter how we define it—the point being, it is not imperative or critical to define it. Labels are just that, a means of communicating a rough description, at best, of the music. Folk music, in and of itself, has no boundaries because it is found in all of us, in our cultures and heritages.

Listen to polka music or to the fiddle tunes that backdrop many children's cartoons or to the exciting music we delight in when we all declare ourselves Irish with the wearing of the green on St. Patrick's Day. Think about your ancestors from three or four hundred years ago who sang the same hymns that you do in your house of worship. Sexual orientation issues have joined racial

---

[1]November 20, 2007.

ones as topical songs, keeping folk current and relevant. The next time you see striking workers on a picket line, think about Woody Guthrie, Pete Seeger, and the countless others who impassioned such efforts—and who stood up for the right to do so, bucking the system and becoming ostracized by our own government. Had they not done so, would our country be as forward-thinking as it is today?

As guardians of folk music, we are curators of our culture. This is the living tradition of folk music. It is the music of our lives—and that of future generations. By passing down the music, we ensure culture, heritage, and the arts.

As demonstrated by the Michael Jackson example alone, folk music can connect with today's youth. And because it also reaches back in time, it is attractive to our senior population. With the Internet and other new, ever-evolving means of sharing information and music, we now have an even greater opportunity for preservation of folk music, without any risk of losing the value of its authenticity.

And while some in the music business fear that digital and other electronic technology will take away from the earnings potential of musicians and songwriters, others embrace these changes as opportunities to expand and earn . . . once we learn how to maneuver and manage successfully these largely uncharted waters.

There are books and opinions out there that rage on about "academic" dyed-in-the-wool authentic folk versus contemporary artists as well as revivalists. All these facets of folk can coexist. The world is wide. When it comes down to it, constructing fences around a genre does not permit it to breathe and grow. It stifles creativity and ideas. It segregates.

The important lesson to take away from folk music is to participate and to keep it going. Pass it on to your children and your children's children. Create and nurture a sense of community. Embrace diversity. It is not so much what your politics and ideas are, but rather the singing out and sharing of them. Oral tradition is not dead as many would have us believe. It has simply morphed into a new form, a new way of communicating oral tradition digitally.

The April 28, 2008, issue of the *New Yorker* posed an evocative question in Burkhard Bilger's article, "The Last Verse: Is There Any Folk Music Still Out There?" In it, the author discusses the extensive field-recording pursuits of song collectors Art Rosenbaum and Lance Ledbetter. I say as long as there are folk singers and songwriters, no matter their stripes, sharing the music, opening doors to new thought, inviting participation in matters important to society, there is and will be folk music still out there.

The Woody Guthrie Foundation, on its Web site, woodyguthrie.org, states its mission is "to promote, perpetuate, and preserve the social, political, and cultural values that Woody Guthrie contributed to the world through his life, his music, and his work." Woody's daughter Nora elaborated, in an e-mail of September 30, 2008:

Sometimes, the best ideas human beings have enter into society through a folk song. It can be philosophical, political, cultural, spiritual, whatever. Simply put, whatever really needs to be said gets written. Through folk songs, humanity's *most* important ideas are kept alive and, in a brilliantly simple way, passed along from one human being to another, often by-passing whatever current censorship or restrictions exist. "This land was made for you and me," "Where have all the flowers gone?" "The answer is blowing in the wind," "We shall overcome," and on and on. These are thoughts, sung.

Many of us who are involved in folk music think of ourselves more as "coal-holders," aiding the continuous, natural flow of the knowledge that exists in folk music, thereby ensuring the next warm campfire of ideas—whenever it's needed.

More Folk: Selected Resources

A lifetime of living with, enjoying, and working in folk and related music styles has contributed to the research basis and writing of this book. To offer you a wide selection to further explore or rediscover folk music, I have provided a cross-section of colloquial and academic materials, including some for young readers.

Some items may be out of print, where others have found new life in revisions, reissues, and digital downloads. Check your local library for older titles as many can provide interesting historical perspective about folk artists who have come and gone, yet who have left an imprint on folk music. Book publisher and publication dates reflect editions I own, borrowed, or referenced online. Original copyright or publication dates (when known) are shown in parentheses where such dates offer more relevance in historical context to the book being mentioned. Flea markets, auction sites, and community book sales can be a goldmine of old recordings and books.

In a relatively short period of time, the amount of available information—print, audio, and video—has expanded exponentially as a result of digital and communications technology. Folk music is a broad subject, made even more expansive by the ability to reach out and find it virtually anywhere in the United States—or across the globe—on the World Wide Web.

The resources that follow are truly but the tip of the iceberg. Included are those entries I felt most comfortable listing for reliability, diversity, and a balanced overview. Space considerations, subjective selection, and the fact that Web addresses often change (or disappear altogether) in the blink of an eye make this appendix your starting point, not definitive. Making good use of search engines will readily provide you with a mountain of links. While there was a plethora of folk-related Web sites offering information and links to other resources, I attempted to include those that best demonstrated longevity, reliability, and/or updatedness.

When it comes to looking for information about specific artists, you cannot go wrong by relying upon their personally maintained Web sites and profiles on such networking pages as Facebook or MySpace; most offer samples and/or download sales of their music. Listservs, Twitter, blogspot.com, and others will provide additional insight and timely information—your endless skyway to folk music, envisioned—or perhaps foreseen!—by Woody Guthrie.

Finally, nothing compares to experiencing live folk music. Check your local listings for a concert or festival in your area and enjoy!

BOOKS

General History and Reference (Excluding Folk Revival)

African Banjo Echoes in Appalachia: A Study of Folk Traditions
by Cecelia Conway
University of Tennessee Press, 1995

American Indians and Their Music
by Frances Densmore
Kessinger Publishing, 2003 (1926)

American Roots Music
edited by Robert Santelli, Holly George-Warren, Jim Brown
Harry N. Abrams, 2002

Cajun Breakdown: The Emergence of an American-Made Music
by Ryan Andre Brasseaux
Oxford University Press, 2009

Cajun Music: A Reflection of a People, Volume I
compiled and edited by Ann Allen Savoy
Bluebird Press, 1984

Deep Community: Adventures in the Modern Folk Underground
by Scott Alarik
Black Wolf Press, 2003

Folk and Blues: The Encyclopedia
by Irwin Stambler and Lyndon Stambler
Thomas Dunne Books/St. Martin's Press, 2001

Folk Music: A Regional Exploration
by Norm Cohen
Greenwood Publishing, 2005

Folk Music: More than a Song
by Kristin Baggelaar and Donald Milton
Thomas Y. Crowell, 1976

Folk Music: The Basics
by Ronald D. Cohen
Routledge/Taylor & Francis, 2005

From Every Stage: Images of America's Roots Music
by Stephanie P. Ledgin
University Press of Mississippi, 2005

Homegrown Music: Discovering Bluegrass
by Stephanie P. Ledgin
University of Illinois Press, 2006 (Praeger, 2004)

Introducing American Folk Music
by Kip Lornell
Brown and Benchmark, 1993

The Land Where the Blues Began
by Alan Lomax
New Press, 2002 (Pantheon, 1993)

Making People's Music: Moe Asch and Folkways Records
by Peter D. Goldsmith
Smithsonian, 2000

Millennium Folk: American Folk Music Since the Sixties
by Thomas R. Gruning
University of Georgia Press, 2006

Music Cultures in the United States: An Introduction
edited by Ellen Koskoff
Routledge, 2005

The Music of Black Americans: A History
by Eileen Southern
W.W. Norton, 1997 (3rd edition)

Music of the First Nations:
Tradition and Innovation in Native North America
edited by Tara Browner
University of Illinois Press, 2009

Musical Instruments of the Southern Appalachian Mountains
by John Rice Irwin
Schiffer, 1983

The Never-Ending Revival: Rounder Records and the Folk Alliance
by Michael F. Scully
University of Illinois Press, 2008

The NPR Curious Listener's Guide to American Folk
by Kip Lornell
Penguin Group, 2004

Sinful Tunes and Spirituals. Black Folk Music to the Civil War
by Dena J. Epstein
University of Illinois Press, 2003

Southern Music/American Music
by Bill C. Malone and David Stricklin
University Press of Kentucky, 2003 (2nd rev./exp. edition)

*Talking Feet: Buck, Flatfoot and Tap. Solo Southern Dance of the Appala-
chian, Piedmont, and Blue Ridge Mountain Regions*
by Mike Seeger
North Atlantic Books, 1993

Texas-Mexican Conjunto: History of a Working-Class Music
by Manuel H. Peña
University of Texas Press, 1985

Voices of Native America: Instruments and Music
by Douglas Spotted Eagle
Eagle's View Publishing, 1997

Waltz the Hall: The American Play Party
by Alan L. Spurgeon
University Press of Mississippi, 2005

Folk Revival

*Baby, Let Me Follow You Down:
The Illustrated Story of the Cambridge Folk Years*
by Eric Von Schmidt and Jim Rooney
University of Massachusetts Press, 1994 (2nd edition)

Bob Dylan and the Beatles: Volume One of the Best of the Blacklisted Journalist
by Al Aronowitz
1st Books, 2003 (out-of-print)
http://blacklistedjournalist.com for excerpts

Folk Music U.S.A.: The Changing Voice of Protest
by Ronald D. Lankford
Schirmer Books, 2005

Follow the Music. The Life and High Times of Elektra Records in the Great Years of American Pop Culture
by Jac Holzman and Gavan Daws
First Media, 2000

Greenwich Village: The Happy Folk Singing Days, 1950s and 1960s
by Madeline MacNeil and Ralph Lee Smith
Mel Bay Publications, 2008

Music of the Counterculture Era
by James E. Perone
Greenwood Publishing, 2004

Rainbow Quest: The Folk Music Revival and American Society, 1940–1970
by Ronald D. Cohen
University of Massachusetts Press, 2002

Transforming Tradition: Folk Music Revivals Examined
edited by Neil V. Rosenberg
University of Illinois Press, 1993

Turn! Turn! Turn!: The '60s Folk-Rock Revolution
by Richie Unterberger
Backbeat Books, 2002

When We Were Good: The Folk Revival
by Robert Cantwell
Harvard University Press, 1996

Which Side Are You On?
An Inside History of the Folk Music Revival in America
by Dick Weissman
Continuum, 2005

Biographies and Autobiographies
(*Note: some are part narrative/part songbook*)

A Deeper Blue: The Life and Music of Townes Van Zandt
by Robert Earl Hardy
University of North Texas Press, 2008

And a Voice To Sing With: A Memoir
by Joan Baez
Plume 1988 (Simon & Schuster, 2009)

The Autobiography of Donovan: The Hurdy Gurdy Man
by Donovan Leitch
St. Martin's Press, 2007

Bound for Glory
by Woody Guthrie
Penguin Group, 1983 (1943)

Chronicles, Volume One
by Bob Dylan
Simon and Schuster, 2004

The Honor of Your Company
by Tom Paxton
Cherry Lane Music, 2000

How Can I Keep from Singing? The Ballad of Pete Seeger
by David K. Dunaway
Villard, 2008 (Da Capo Press, 1990)

The Life and Legend of Leadbelly
by Charles Wolfe and Kip Lornell
Da Capo Press, 1999

The Life of a Children's Troubadour: An Autobiography
by Raffi
Troubadour Records, 1998

Lonesome Traveler: The Life of Lee Hays
by Doris Willens
University of Nebraska Press, 1993 (W.W. Norton, 1988)

The Mayor of MacDougal Street: A Memoir
by Dave Van Ronk with Elijah Wald
Da Capo Press, 2005

Minstrel of the Appalachians: The Story of Bascom Lamar Lunsford
by Loyal Jones
University Press of Kentucky, 2002

Positively 4th Street: The Lives and Times of Joan Baez, Bob Dylan, Mimi Baez Fariña and Richard Fariña
by David Hajdu
Northpoint Press, 2002

The Protest Singer: An Intimate Portrait of Pete Seeger
by Alec Wilkinson
Knopf, 2009

Ramblin' Man: The Life and Times of Woody Guthrie
by Ed Cray
W.W. Norton, 2004

Singing Family of the Cumberlands
by Jean Ritchie
University Press of Kentucky, 1988 (1955)

Society's Child: My Autobiography
by Janis Ian
Tarcher/Penguin Group, 2008

Steve Goodman: Facing the Music
by Clay Eals
ECW Press, 2007

"To Everything There Is a Season": Pete Seeger and the Power of Song
by Allan M. Winkler
Oxford University Press, 2009

Trust Your Heart: An Autobiography
by Judy Collins
Houghton Mifflin, 1987

Where Have All the Flowers Gone: A Musical Autobiography
by Pete Seeger
Sing Out! Publications, 1997
Earlier edition of the one below

Where Have All the Flowers Gone: A Singalong Memoir
by Pete Seeger
Sing Out! Publications, 2009

*Will You Miss Me When I'm Gone? The Carter Family
and Their Legacy in American Music*
by Mark Zwonitzer with Charles Hirshberg
Simon and Schuster, 2002

Woody Guthrie: A Life
by Joe Klein
Dell, 1999

Songbooks
(*Note: some are part narrative/part songbook*)

American Ballads and Folk Songs
by John A. Lomax and Alan Lomax
Dover Publications, 1994 (MacMillan, 1934)

The American Songbag
by Carl Sandburg
Houghton Mifflin Harcourt, 1990 (1927)

Backpocket Old-Time Songbook
by Wayne Erbsen
Native Ground Music, 2007

The Ballad Book of John Jacob Niles
by John Jacob Niles
University Press of Kentucky, 2000

The Books of American Negro Spirituals, Two Volumes in One
by James Weldon Johnson and J. Rosamond Johnson
Da Capo Press, 2002 (1925)

*The Collected Reprints from Sing Out!
The Folk Song Magazine, Volumes 1–6: 1959–1964*
Sing Out! Publications, 1990

80 Appalachian Folk Songs
collected by Cecil Sharp and Maud Karpeles
edited by Maud Karpeles
Faber and Faber, 1983 (1968)

The English and Scottish Popular Ballads, 5 Volume Set
by Francis James Child
Dover Publications, 2003

Essential Bluegrass & Old-Time Songbook: 50 Songs You Need to Know
by Scott Atkinson
World Street Press, 2008
http://worldstreetpress.com

Folk Songs of the Southern Appalachians
by Jean Ritchie, Ron Pen, and Alan Lomax
University Press of Kentucky, 1997

The Folksong Fake Book
Hal Leonard Corporation, 2001

Great Songs of Folk Music
edited by Milton Okun
Cherry Lane Music, 2007

Hymns of the Old Camp Ground
by Wayne Erbsen
Native Ground Music, 2009

Our Singing Country: Folk Songs and Ballads
collected and compiled by John A. Lomax and Alan Lomax
Dover Publications, 2000 unabridged (Macmillan, 1941)

The People's Song Book
edited by Waldemar Hille
Oak Publications, 2007 (Boni and Gaer, 1948)

Rise Up Singing: The Group Singing Songbook
edited by Peter Blood and Annie Patterson
Sing Out! Publications, 2004

Sing for Freedom: The Story of the Civil Rights Movement through Its Songs
by Guy and Candie Carawan
NewSouth Books, 2008

Too Many Songs
by Tom Lehrer
Pantheon Books, 1981

Traditional American Folk Songs from the Anne & Frank Warner Collection
by Anne Warner
Syracuse University Press, 1984

A Treasury of Stephen Foster
Random House, 1946

FOLKLIFE CENTERS, COLLECTIONS, AND DIGITAL ARCHIVES
(*Note: a visit may require an appointment; call ahead.*)

Alan Lomax Archive and the Association for Cultural Equity
450 West 41 Street, 6th Floor
New York NY 10036
212-268-4623
http://lomaxarchive.com

American Folklife Center
Library of Congress
101 Independence Avenue SE
Washington DC 20540
202-707-5510
http://loc.gov/folklife/

Archives of Traditional Music
Indiana University
Morrison Hall 117 & 120
Bloomington IN 47405
812-855-4679
http://www.indiana.edu/~libarchm/

Broadside, The Topical Song Magazine
http://broadsidemagazine.com
(entire archive, issues 1–186, 1962–1988)

Center for Southern Folklore
119 South Main Street
Memphis TN 38103
901-525-3655
http://southernfolklore.com

Center for Traditional Music and Dance Archives
32 Broadway, Suite 1314
New York NY 10004
212-571-1555 x27
http://ctmd.org/archives.htm

Digital Library of Appalachia
http://aca-dla.org

Folk Music Index to Recordings
http://ibiblio.org/folkindex/

Folkstreams.net
http://folkstreams.net

McGuinn's Folk Den
http://www.ibiblio.org/jimmy/folkden/php/search/

The Mudcat Cafe and Digital Tradition
http://mudcat.org

New Hampshire Library of Traditional Music and Dance
University of New Hampshire Library
18 Library Way
Durham NH 03824
603-862-1535
http://www.library.unh.edu/special/index.php/category/folk-music-dance

New York Public Library for the Performing Arts
40 Lincoln Center Plaza
New York NY 10023
212-870-1630
http://nypl.org/research/lpa/lpa.html

Old Town School of Folk Music Resource Center
4544 North Lincoln Avenue
Chicago IL 60625
773-728-6000
http://oldtownschool.org

Sing Out! Resource Center
(call for location and appointment)
Bethlehem PA
888-SING-OUT
610-865-5366
http://singout.org/sorce.html

Smithsonian Center for Folklife and Cultural Heritage
Ralph Rinzler Folklife Archives and Collections
Capital Gallery Building
600 Maryland Avenue SW
Suite 2001 MRC 520
Washington DC 20024
202-633-6440
http://folklife.si.edu

Southern Folklife Collection
Wilson Library
University of North Carolina
Chapel Hill NC 27514
919-962-1345
http://www.lib.unc.edu/mss/sfc1/

The Traditional Ballad Index
http://www.csufresno.edu/folklore/BalladIndexTOC.html

UCLA Ethnomusicology Archive
1630 Schoenberg Music Building
Los Angeles CA 90095
310-825-1695
http://ethnomusic.ucla.edu/archive/

Western Folklife Center
501 Railroad Street
Elko NV 89801
775-738-7508
http://westernfolklife.org

Woody Guthrie Foundation and Archives
250 West 57 Street, Suite 1218
New York NY 10107
212-541-6230
http://woodyguthrie.org

VIEWING ROOM: RANDOM PICKS

This list offers historical television programs, documentary films, and commercial fiction, among others. Original film release date, when known, is in parentheses following title. All are available in DVD format, unless otherwise noted. Label information and either catalog number or DVD release date are indicated, where known. A Web address is given where it is the only source for a product. YouTube.com and other sites link hundreds of clips, fan-made to professionally done, from house concert footage to festivals. In addition, many, if not most, major artists have concert DVDs available as well.

A Mighty Wind (2003)
directed by Christopher Guest
Warner Home Video, 2003

A Musical Journey: The Films of Pete, Toshi & Dan Seeger 1957–1964
Vestapol 13042

Appalachian Journey
by Alan Lomax
http://media-generation.com

Awake My Soul: The Story of the Sacred Harp
by Matt and Erica Hinton
Awake Productions, 2008

The Ballad of Greenwich Village (2005)
directed by Karen Kramer
Erzulie Films, 2005
http://balladofgreenwichvillage.com

The Ballad of Ramblin' Jack
directed by Aiyana Elliott
Winstar, 2000

The Best of Hootenanny
Shout Factory 826663-10220

Bob Dylan: Don't Look Back (1967)
directed by D.A. Pennebaker
Docurama, 2007

Bob Dylan: The Other Side of the Mirror—Live at the Newport Folk Festival 1963–1965
directed by Murray Lerner
Sony, 2007

Bound for Glory (1976)
directed by Hal Ashby
MGM, 2000

Dreams and Songs of the Noble Old
by Alan Lomax
http://media-generation.com

"Festival!" (1967)
directed by Murray Lerner
Eagle Vision Media, 2005

Four American Roots Music Films
by Yasha Aginsky
Vestapol 13103

Georgia Sea Island Singers (1964)
by Bess Lomax Hawes
http://media-generation.com

Legends of Old-Time Music
Vestapol 13026

Midnight Special: The Life of Lead Belly
Film House, 2010 *forthcoming*
http://filmhouse.com

New England Fiddles/New England Dances
by John Bishop and Nicholas Hawes
http://media-generation.com

The New Lost City Ramblers in Always Been a Rambler
directed by Yasha Aginsky
Arhoolie, 2009

No Direction Home: Bob Dylan (2005)
directed by Martin Scorsese
Paramount, 2005

Pete Seeger: The Power of Song (2007)
directed by Jim Brown
Miriam Collection, 2008

*Rainbow Quest: The Clancy Brothers and Tommy Makem with Tom Paxton/
Mamou Cajun Band*
by Pete Seeger
Shanachie 609

Rainbow Quest: Judy Collins and Elizabeth Cotten
by Pete Seeger
Shanachie 610

Sets in Order Presents Square Dancing (1950s)
directed by Bob Osgood
online clip
http://avgeeks.com

Songcatcher (2000)
directed by Maggie Greenwald
Lions Gate, 2003

Talking Feet: Solo Southern Dance. Flatfoot, Buck and Tap
by Mike Seeger
Smithsonian Folkways, 2007

To Hear Your Banjo Play (1947)
directed by Irving Lerner and Willard Van Dyke
online clip
http://avgeeks.com

The Weavers: Wasn't That a Time! (1982)
Warner Reprise, 1992 (VHS out-of-print)

Why Old Time?
directed by Chris Valluzzo and Sean Kotz
Horse Archer Productions, 2009
http://whyoldtime.com

MUSEUMS
   (*The following exhibit various degrees and types of folk music content.*)

Blue Ridge Institute and Museum
Ferrum College
20 Museum Drive
Ferrum VA 24088
540-365-4416
http://blueridgeinstitute.org

Blues and Legends Hall of Fame Museum
http://bluesmuseum.org
Relocating at press time

Country Music Hall of Fame and Museum
222 Fifth Avenue South
Nashville TN 37203
615-416-2001
http://countrymusichalloffame.com

Delta Blues Museum
#1 Blues Alley
Clarksdale MS 38614
662-627-6820
http://deltabluesmuseum.org

International Bluegrass Music Museum
117 Daviess Street
Owensboro KY 42303
888-MY BANJO
270-926-7891
http://bluegrassmuseum.org

The Martin Guitar Museum and Visitors Center
510 Sycamore Street
Nazareth PA 18064
610-759-2837
http://martinguitar.com/visit/museum.html

The Museum at Bethel Woods
200 Hurd Road
Swan Lake NY 12783
866-781-2922
http://bethelwoodscenter.org/museum.aspx

Museum of Appalachia
2819 Andersonville Highway
Clinton TN 37716
865-494-7680
http://museumofappalachia.org

The Museum of Musical Instruments
http://themomi.org

Musical Instrument Museum
4725 East Mayo Boulevard
Phoenix AZ 85050
480-478-6000
http://themim.org
Opening April 24, 2010

National Music Museum
University of South Dakota
414 East Clark Street
Vermillion SD 57069
605-677-5306
http://usd.edu/smm

Pioneer Music Museum
Main Street
Anita IA 50020
712-762-4363

Rock and Roll Hall of Fame and Museum
1100 Rock and Roll Boulevard
East Ninth Street at Lake Erie
Cleveland OH 44114
216-781-ROCK
http://rockhall.com

Ukulele Hall of Fame and Museum
http://ukulele.org

KEEPING CURRENT

Publications

Traditional print publications are becoming few and far between. Many are transitioning to online presence only. Others are reinventing what they are offering in the way of folk news, reviews, interviews, and tour dates, while some are opting to host blogs, tweets, and other discussion forums, including news groups and listservs. The following represents an array of publications and Web sites with national coverage and focus; there are numerous local and regional ones not included here.

Spotlight: *Sing Out!* magazine remains the gold standard for folk songs and folk music coverage. Founded in 1950, the quarterly publication preserves folk music's storied past while providing a window to today's folk music scene, with a solid nod toward the future. At its core is the basic idea of participation; its mission statement is "to preserve and support the cultural diversity and heritage of all traditional and contemporary folk musics, and to encourage making folk music a part of our everyday lives."

Its origins grew out of a post–World War II organization, People's Songs, Inc., formed by such artists as Woody Guthrie, Pete Seeger, Paul Robeson, Alan Lomax, and others, who initiated publication of the *People's Songs* newsletter to "create, promote, and distribute songs of labor and the American people." While *People's Songs* didn't survive, a similar endeavor was undertaken. May 1950 saw publication of the first issue of *Sing Out!,* the name taken from a line in "The Hammer Song," written by Pete Seeger and Lee Hays.

Today the magazine is the core of Sing Out! Inc., a tax-exempt, nonprofit, educational organization, which also publishes songbooks and maintains a resource center. Each issue of *Sing Out!* is chock full of articles, news, reviews, commentary and analysis of traditional and contemporary folk music in its broad range of definition, complete lead sheets for 20 songs, plus those songs on an accompanying CD sampler.

About.com: Folk Music
http://folkmusic.about.com

AcousticMusic.net
http://acousticmusic.net

AcousticMusicScene.com
http://acousticmusicscene.com

Ballad Tree: A Guide to Folk Music Online
http://balladtree.com

Bluegrass Music Profiles
PO Box 850
Nicholasville KY 40340
859-333-6465
http://bluegrassmusicprofiles.com

Bluegrass Unlimited
PO Box 771
Warrenton VA 20188
800-BLU-GRAS
540-349-8181
http://bluegrassmusic.com

Blues Revue
Route 1, Box 75
Salem WV 26426
304-782-1971
http://bluesrevue.com

Cybergrass
http://cybergrass.com

Dirty Linen
PO Box 66600
Baltimore MD 21239
410-583-7973
http://dirtylinen.com

Folk Library Index
http://www.folklib.net/first_time.shtml

FolkWax
http://folkwax.com

Folkways Magazine
http://folkways.si.edu/magazine/

Living Blues Magazine
PO Box 1848
1111 Jackson Avenue West
University MS 38677
http://livingblues.com

Music Matters Review
http://mmreview.com

No Depression
http://nodepression.net

The Old-Time Herald
PO Box 61679
Durham NC 27715
919-286-2041
http://oldtimeherald.org

Puremusic
http://puremusic.com

RootsWorld
http://www.rootsworld.com/rw/

Sing Out!
PO Box 5460
Bethlehem PA 18015
888-SING-OUT
610-865-5366
http://singout.org

Miscellaneous Online Community Resources

http://efolkmusic.org
http://folk.jg.org
http://hickorywind.org

NATIONAL AND INTERNATIONAL ORGANIZATIONS

Americana Music Association
PO Box 128077
Nashville TN 37212
615-386-6936
http://americanamusic.org

The Blues Foundation
49 Union Avenue
Memphis TN 38103
901-527-2583
http://blues.org

The Children's Music Network
PO Box 1341
Evanston IL 60204
847-673-2243
http://cmnonline.org

Country Dance and Song Society
PO Box 338
Haydenville MA 01039
413-268-7426
http://cdss.org

Country Music Association
One Music Circle South
Nashville TN 37203
615-244-2840
http://cmaworld.com

Folk Alliance International
510 South Main, First Floor
Memphis TN 38103
901-522-1170
http://folk.org

International Bluegrass Music Association
2 Music Circle South, Suite 100
Nashville TN 37203
888-438-4262
615-256-3222
http://ibma.org

International Native American and World Flute Association
3351 Mintonville Point Drive
Suffolk VA 23435
757-538-0468
http://worldflutes.org

National Traditional Country Music Association
PO Box 492
Anita IA 50020
712-762-4363

People's Music Network for Songs of Freedom and Struggle
c/o Diane Crowe
78 Cave Hill Road
Leverett MA 01054
413-548-9394
http://peoplesmusic.org

LIVE FOLK!

House concerts, intimate clubs, large concert halls, and festivals—all provide wonderful opportunities for live folk music, performed by local as well as internationally renowned musicians. Check event listings in your community newspaper or online calendar, or refer to any of the references cited in the Keeping Current section to locate those close to home; many publications carry their own schedules of concerts, festivals, open mics, songwriter circles, and jam sessions. Local folk music and dance organizations typically publish event calendars as well. See the final section of this resource guide for a jump start at connecting with a folk music or dance association in your area. And, of course, virtually all artists maintain appearance dates on their personal Web sites or social networking pages.

The Internet sites listed below offer additional opportunities to locate folk music and dance events of every size, shape, and format, from community concerts to multiday festivals, featuring a full range of performance, workshops, dance, and children's activities.

http://concertsinyourhome.com
http://festivalfinder.com
http://festivals.com
http://folkjam.org
http://musi-cal.com
http://thedancegypsy.com

TURN YOUR RADIO ON

As Albert E. Brumley wrote in the old-time gospel song, "Turn your radio on and listen to the music in the air." Nowadays, the concept of "radio" has taken on meanings far beyond a tabletop appliance or even a high-end sound system. Where and how to tune in to radio broadcasts is changing rapidly. Traditional radio, now sometimes referred to as "terrestrial" radio, most certainly has not been rendered obsolete; rather it has expanded its reach. Traditional radio stations often stream live or rebroadcast over the Internet as well, sometimes using a third-party Internet radio streaming site. And satellite radio beams globally, from your car, from your home, just about any place you go; it can go.

Historically, most folk music programming has emanated from stations at the low end of the FM dial. These are largely public radio and university- or college-operated stations where formats and advertising dollars are not the driving forces behind programming. Folk music will often fall under several guises, including roots music, Americana, or acoustic music, in addition to specialty shows devoted to blues, bluegrass, honky-tonk country, among others. Internet and satellite radio also offer original programming (hint: look under "country" to find folk-related programming). Other genres or categories in which to discover folk music are "world" and "children's" programming. Last but not least, podcasts provide yet another option for both audio and video broadcasting.

There are hundreds of local folk music programs, along with a dizzying array of syndicated ones. Many of the publications listed earlier maintain radio-show listings. One great place to start is the *FOLKDJ-L,* an electronic discussion group for DJs and other people interested in folk-based music on the radio. One does not have to be a radio host to subscribe to the listserv.

Deserving special recognition as the longest-running folk music program—as well as one of the longest-running radio shows of any kind—in the world, Oscar Brand's *Folksong Festival* premiered on December 10, 1945, on WNYC AM, New York City. In 1995, on its 50th anniversary, the program earned a personal Peabody Award for the visionary folk performer, an honor also won that year by Oprah Winfrey. In addition to Brand's extensive list of folk music credits in performance and on radio and television, he has written for Broadway and was on the panel that created *Sesame Street.*

Another American staple of radio was memorialized on film in director Robert Altman's 2006 *A Prairie Home Companion,* with real life host Garrison Keillor as himself. The weekly live show, syndicated throughout the country, features an eclectic range of folk performers, among other genres.

FOLKDJ-L
http://folkradio.org

Folksong Festival
http://wnyc.org/shows/folksong

A Prairie Home Companion
http://prairiehome.publicradio.org

Folk Radio-Show Directories

http://radiofolk.org

http://publicradiofan.com/cgibin/statsearch.pl?format=folk&lang=

Internet Radio Hosting Sites

http://live365.com

http://virtualtuner.com

http://vtuner.com

Satellite Radio

Sirius XM Satellite Radio
The Village (Host Mary Sue Twohy, others)
http://siriusxm.com

Selected Internet-Only Radio Stations, Programs, Podcasts

http://downhomeradioshow.com

http://folkalley.com

http://www.homegrownradionj.com

http://internetfolkfestival.com

http://wholewheatradio.org

Selected Syndicated Programs

American Routes with Nick Spitzer
http://americanroutes.org

Celtic Connections with Bryan Kelso Crow
http://celticconnectionsradio.org

The Folk Sampler with Mike Flynn
http://folksampler.com

Mountain Stage with Larry Groce
http://www.mountainstage.org

River City Folk with Tom May
http://tommayfolk.com/rivercityfolk

The Sing Out! Radio Magazine with Matt Watroba
http://singout.org

The Thistle and Shamrock
http://thistleradio.com

WoodSongs Old-Time Radio Hour with Michael Johnathon
http://woodsongs.com

World Café with David Dye
http://xpn.org/xpn-programs/world-cafe

THE LEARNING PLACE

Instructional Materials

Hal Leonard Corporation
414-774-3630
http://halleonard.com

Homespun Music Instruction
800-338-2737
845-246-2550
http://homespun.com

How to Play the 5-String Banjo
by Pete Seeger
Oak Publications, 2006 (1948)

Mel Bay Publications
800-8-MELBAY
636-257-3970
http://melbay.com

Stefan Grossman's Guitar Workshop
973-729-5544
http://guitarvideos.com

Songwriting

Songwriting and the Creative Process
by Steve Gillette
Sing Out! Publications, 1995

The Songwriter's Handbook
by Tom T. Hall
Thomas Nelson, 2001

Instrument/Instructional Publications

Acoustic Guitar
415-485-6946
http://acousticguitar.com

The Autoharp Page
http://autoharp.org

Autoharp Quarterly
206-439-3549 or 800-630-HARP
http://autoharpquarterly.com

Banjo Newsletter
800-759-7425
410-263-6503
508-645-3648
http://banjonews.com

The Celtic Harp Page
http://celticharper.com

Dulcimer Players News
423-886-3966
http://dpnews.com

Everything Dulcimer
http://everythingdulcimer.com

ezFolk
http://ezfolk.com

Fiddler Magazine
902-794-2558
http://fiddle.com

Flatpicking Guitar Magazine
800-413-8296
540-980-0338
http://flatpick.com

Flea Market Music for All Things Ukulele
http://www.fleamarketmusic.com

Harmonica Lessons
http://harmonicalessons.com

Jew's Harp Guild
http://jewsharpguild.org

Mandolin Magazine
503-364-2100
http://mandolinmagazine.com

MandoZine
http://mandozine.com

Academic Programs and Camps

Appalshop
91 Madison Avenue
Whitesburg KY 41858
606-633-0108
http://appalshop.org

Augusta Heritage Center
Davis and Elkins College
Hermanson Campus Center
100 Campus Drive
Elkins WV 26241
800-624-3157 x1209
304-637-1209
http://augustaheritage.com

Bluegrass, Old-Time, and Country Music Program
Center for Appalachian Studies and Services
East Tennessee State University
PO Box 70435
Johnson City TN 37614
423-439-7072
http://etsu.edu/cass/bluegrass/

Camp Fasola
Held at Camp McDowell
Nauvoo AL 35578
404-237-1246
http://fasola.org/camp

Catskills Irish Arts Week
East Durham NY 12423
518-634-2286
http://irishvillageusa.com

Common Ground on the Hill
2 College Hill
Westminster MD 21157
410-857-2771
http://commongroundonthehill.org

fiddlekids
Bobbi Nikles, Director
c/o Freight & Salvage Coffeehouse
1111 Addison Street
Berkeley CA 94702
510-848-2112
http://fiddlekids.com

John C. Campbell Folk School
One Folk School Road
Brasstown NC 28902
800-FOLKSCH
828-837-2775
http://folkschool.org

Mark O'Connor String Camps
PO Box 110573
Nashville TN 37222
615-941-7426
http://markoconnor.com

Mars Hill College Music Weeks
Conferences and Events
PO Box 370
Mars Hill NC 28754
828-689-1167
http://www.mhc.edu/administration/events/

Ozark Folk School
1032 Park Avenue
Mountain View AR 72560
800-264-3655
870-269-3851
http://ozarkfolkcenter.com

Pinewoods Camp
80 Cornish Field Road
Plymouth MA 02360
508-224-4858
http://pinewoods.org

SummerSongs
PO Box 803
Saugerties NY 12477
845-247-7049
http://summersongs.com

Swannanoa Gathering
Warren Wilson College
701 Warren Wilson Road
Swannanoa NC 28778
828-298-3434
http://swangathering.com

KIDSTUFF: A POTPOURRI

Books

All Night, All Day: A Child's First Book of African-American Spirituals
selected and illustrated by Ashley Bryan
Simon and Schuster Children's Publishing, 2003

American Folk Songs for Children
by Ruth Crawford Seeger, illustrated by Barbara Cooney
Music Sales, 2002 (1948)

The Deaf Musicians
story by Pete Seeger and Paul Dubois Jacobs,
illustrated by R. Gregory Christie
Penguin Group, 2006

Folk
by Richard Carlin
Facts on File, 2005

From Sea to Shining Sea. A Treasury of American Folklore and Folk Songs
compiled by Amy L. Cohn
Scholastic, 1993

Home on the Range: John A. Lomax and His Cowboy Songs
by Deborah Hopkinson, illustrated by S. D. Schindler
Penguin Group, 2009

150 American Folk Songs to Sing, Read and Play
selected and edited by Peter Erdei, collected principally by Katalin Komlos
Boosey and Hawkes, 2004

Pete Seeger's Storytelling Book
composed by Pete Seeger and Paul Dubois Jacobs
Harcourt, 2000

This Land Is Your Land
words and music by Woody Guthrie, paintings by Kathy Jakobsen
Little, Brown Young Readers, 2008 (1998)

This Land Was Made for You and Me: The Life and Songs of Woody Guthrie
by Elizabeth Partridge
Penguin Group, 2002

Music

Tom Chapin. *Family Tree* (Gadfly 801)

Mike Cross. *Michael's Magic Music Box* (http://mikecross.com)

Down at the Sea Hotel. A Greg Brown song illustrated by Mireille Levert. Singer-songwriter lullabies performed by John Gorka, Eliza Gilkyson, Lucy Kaplansky, Guy Davis, Lynn Miles and the Wailin' Jennys (The Secret Mountain 33540)

Jonathan Edwards, Cathy Fink, John McCutcheon, Larry Penn, Phil & Naomi Rosenthal. *Grandma's Patchwork Quilt* (American Melody 4103)

John Foley's Radar Rangers. *Short Folk Songs (for Short Folks)* (http://cdbaby.com/cd/radarrangers)

Si Kahn. *Good Times and Bedtimes* (Rounder download)

John Kirk and Trish Miller. *The Big Rock Candy Mountain* (Gentle Wind 768454106722)

John McCutcheon. *Mail Myself to You* (Rounder 8016)

Ellis Paul. *The Dragonfly Races* (Black Wolf 2290)

Tom Paxton. *Your Shoes, My Shoes* (Red House 152)

Peter, Bethany and Rufus. *Puff & Other Family Classics* (http://peterbethanyandrufus.com)

Peter, Paul and Mary. *Peter, Paul and Mommy* (Warner Brothers/WEA 1785)

Raffi. *Songs of Our World* (Rounder 8146)

Phil Rosenthal & Family. *The Green Grass Grew All Around* (American Melody 5115)

Mike and Peggy Seeger. *American Folk Songs for Children* (Rounder 8001)

Pete Seeger. *Folk Songs for Young People* (Smithsonian Folkways 45024)

Sing Along with Putumayo [various artists] (Putumayo Kids 222)

Doc Watson. *Sings Songs for Little Pickers. Live!* (Sugar Hill 3786, reissued Alcazar 1005)

Video Instruction

Cathy Fink and Marcy Marxer. *Making and Playing Homemade Instruments* (Homespun MAXHM21)

Marcy Marxer. *Kids' Guitar* (Homespun MAXKI23)

AUDIO/VIDEO RECORDING LABELS

In folk music, it is often preferred, when possible, that you buy an artist's music from the performer, either at a personal appearance or from the musician's Web or social networking site. This ensures more money goes directly to the artist. Many folk artists record for small, independent labels. Some companies specialize in reissues of archival or out-of-print recordings. Many of the following also produce concert DVDs or those of historical, documentary nature. Many are beginning to move to digital downloads in MP3 format, a continuing trend among a greater number of labels and artists.

American Melody Recordings
203-457-0881
http://americanmelody.com

Appleseed Recordings
610-701-5755
http://appleseedrec.com

Arhoolie Records
510-525-7471
http://arhoolie.com

Bear Family Records
49-4748-82160 (Germany)
http://bear-family.de

Canyon Records
800-268-1141
http://canyonrecords.com

Compass Records
615-320-7672
http://compassrecords.com

Dust-to-Digital
http://dust-digital.com

Field Recorders' Collective
http://fieldrecorder.com

Folk Era Records
630-637-2303
http://folkera.com

Folk-Legacy Records
800-836-0901
http://folk-legacy.com

Gadfly Records
802-865-2406
http://gadflyrecords.com

June Appal Records
606-633-0108
http://appalshop.org

Media-Generation
503-233-4047
http://media-generation.com

Native Ground Music
800-752-2656
828-299-7031
http://nativeground.com

Red House Records
800-695-4687
651-644-4161
http://redhouserecords.com

Revenant Records
http://revenantrecords.com

Righteous Babe Records
800-ON-HER-OWN
716-852-8020
http://righteousbabe.com

Rounder Records
800-ROUNDER
617-354-0700
http://rounder.com

Shanachie Records
800-497-1043
973-579-7763
http://shanachie.com

Smithsonian Folkways Recordings
888-FOLKWAYS
202-633-6450
http://folkways.si.edu

Strictly Country Records
31-297-347-101 (The Netherlands)
540-982-6900 (USA)
http://strictlycountryrecords.com

Sugar Hill Records
http://sugarhillrecords.com

Vanguard Records
310-829-9355
http://vanguardrecords.com

Vestapol Videos
973-729-5544
http://guitarvideos.com/vesta/00vesta.htm

Waterbug Records
630-534-6063
http://waterbug.com

Yazoo Records
800-497-1043
http://yazoorecords.com

Other Retail Outlets with Folk Product

Elderly Instruments
888-473-5810
517-372-7890
http://www.elderly.com

Lark in the Morning
877-964-5569
http://larkinthemorning.com

Rhino Records
888-440-4232
http://rhino.com

Shout! Factory
http://shoutfactory.com

Village Records
http://villagerecords.com

CLOSE TO HOME

It is impossible to include the hundreds, if not thousands, of local and regional folk music and dance organizations, performance venues, and festivals located around the United States. In an attempt to whet your appetite, I have included a random listing of one folk entity or endeavor for each of the 50 states plus Washington DC. Contacting any of these to inquire about others that exist in a specific area of your state is another route to take to find similar venues and organizations. The vast majority of folk organizations and events are still run by a faithful, tireless core of volunteers. Keep that in mind as you discover folk music wherever it takes you.

Alabama
Sacred Harp Singing
http://fasola.org

Alaska
Alaska Folk Festival
http://akfolkfest.org
907-463-3316

Arizona
Flagstaff Friends of Traditional Music
http://ffotm.net

Arkansas
Little Rock Folk Club
http://lrfolkclub.org

California
California Traditional Music Society
http://ctmsfolkmusic.org
818-817-7756

Colorado
Swallow Hill Music Association
http://swallowhill.com
303-777-1003, 877-214-7013

Connecticut
CT Folk
http://ctfolk.com

Delaware
Delaware Friends of Folk
http://delfolk.org
877-DEL-FOLK

District of Columbia
World Folk Music Association
http://wfma.net
202-362-2225

Florida
Friends of Florida Folk
http://foff.org

Georgia
Atlanta Area Friends of Folk Music
http://aaffm.org

Hawaii
Big Island Contra Dances
http://contradancehawaii.com

Idaho
National Oldtime Fiddlers' Contest and Festival
http://fiddlecontest.com

Illinois
Old Town School of Folk Music
http://oldtownschool.org
773-728-6000

Indiana
Central Indiana Folk Music and Mountain Dulcimer Society
http://indianafolkmusic.org

Iowa
Oak Tree Opry
http://oldtimemusic.tipzu.com/oak-tree-opry
712-762-4363

Kansas
West Side Folk
http://westsidefolk.org
785-865-FOLK

Kentucky
Master Musicians Festival
http://mastermusiciansfestival.com
606-677-2933

Louisiana
Louisiana Folk Roots
http://lafolkroots.org
337-234-8360

Maine
Stone Mountain Arts Center
http://stonemountainartscenter.com
866-227-6523

Maryland
Baltimore Folk Music Society
http://bfms.org
410-366-0808

Massachusetts
Folk Song Society of Greater Boston
http://fssgb.org
617-623-1806

Michigan
Folk Music Society of Midland
http://folkmusicsociety.org

Minnesota
Bothy Folk Club
http://bothy.org

Mississippi
Sunflower River Blues and Gospel Festival
http://sunflowerfest.org

Missouri
CrossCurrents, Kansas City Folk Arts Alliance
http://crosscurrentsculture.org
816-292-2887

Montana
Montana State Oldtime Fiddlers Association
http://montanafiddlers.org

Nebraska
Lincoln Association for Traditional Arts (LAFTA)
http://lafta.net

Nevada
Sierra Contra Dance Society
http://sierracontra.org

New Hampshire
Peterborough Folk Music Society
http://pfmsconcerts.org
603-827-2905

New Jersey
Folk Project of New Jersey
http://folkproject.org

New Mexico
New Mexico Folk Music and Dance Society (FolkMADS)
http://folkmads.org

New York
Folk Music Society of NY (NY Pinewoods Folk Music Club)
http://minstrelrecords.com/fmsny
718-672-6399

North Carolina
PineCone, Piedmont Council of Traditional Music
http://pinecone.org
919-664-8333

North Dakota
The Listening Room
http://thelisteningroomfargo.com
701-237-0230

Ohio
Folknet, NE Ohio Folk & Traditional Music & Dance Society
http://folknet.org
216-556-3820

Oklahoma
Woody Guthrie Folk Festival
http://woodyguthrie.com
918-623-2440

Oregon
Portland FolkMusic Society
http://portlandfolkmusic.org

Pennsylvania
Philadelphia Folksong Society
http://pfs.org
215-247-1300

Rhode Island
Stone Soup Folk Arts Foundation
http://stonesoupcoffeehouse.com
401-921-5115

South Carolina
Dry Ridge Productions
http://dryridge.org
864-963-8688

South Dakota
South Dakota Friends of Traditional Music
http://fotm.org
605-987-2582

Tennessee
Jubilee Community Arts
http://jubileearts.org
865-522-5851

Texas
Austin Friends of Traditional Music
http://aftm.us

Utah
Bridger Folk Music Society
http://bridgerfolk.org

Vermont
Champlain Valley Folk Festival
http://cvfest.org
877-850-0206

Virginia
Tidewater Friends of Folk Music
http://tffm.org
757-626-FOLK

Washington
Northwest Folklife
http://nwfolklife.org

West Virginia
West Virginia State Folk Festival
http://wvfolkfestival.org

Wisconsin
Madison Folk Music Society
http://madfolk.org

Wyoming
Wyoming Old-Time Fiddle Association
http://wyomingfiddle.org

Listening Space: A Folk Continuum

Probably every author writing an introductory book about a particular music genre faces the identical question—what to include in a reference guide to recordings, that is, "must-haves," "favorites," "classic picks," or something else. Since the path I have chosen in writing *Discovering Folk Music* is one that explores its many twists and turns, I have opted to pull titles from my stacks that represent the folk music continuum, from traditional to folk revival artists to singer-songwriters to folk-rock innovators. Rather than aim for 25 or 50 albums, I simply went through a vast collection and started pulling titles that have "wow" appeal and/or historical significance. Some on this list are substitute versions I have found more readily available than the originals, since some that I chose are out of print. Others are going . . . and coming soon digitally as this book goes to press!

Digital downloads and "on demand" releases are reviving many of the older titles, as well as becoming the sole choice for many artists' recordings. While some on this list may no longer be available, they may lead you to others by the same artist—or may become available again as digital downloads expand. As suggested previously, flea markets, library sales, and online auction sites are often gold mines for out-of-print items.

Labels and catalog numbers have become a bit confusing, even moot in some cases, as often there are a variety of reissue versions, even on different labels. For this information, I relied on the artist or record label's Web site, when available.

A final thought on this potpourri of folk and folk-related albums. . . . It struck me as I sampled cuts from older recordings how full circle folk music has come from the pivotal sixties' folk era. Listening to such seminal artists—not typically thought of as "folk" in today's view—as Simon and Garfunkel, John Denver, or Harry Chapin, for example, and fast forwarding to the music of

21st-century "new folk" artists, I found that there is not much difference in
what made these performers stand out from others as with those now on the
horizon. Just as the precocious stable of performers 40 to 50 years ago expanded on their original songs with arrangements beyond voice and acoustic
guitar, so, too, are today's outstanding performers pushing the envelope.

David Amram. *Southern Stories* (Chrome 4202)
Anthology of American Folk Music, edited by Harry Smith [various artists] (Smith-
      sonian Folkways 40090)
*Art of Field Recording, Volume I: 50 Years of Traditional American Music Docu-
      mented by Art Rosenbaum* [various artists] (Dust-to-Digital 08)
Joan Baez. *From Every Stage* (A&M 6506)
Harry Belafonte. *Live in Concert at the Carnegie Hall* (RCA Victor Europe
      115713)
   Caution: The U.S. re-release of the classic 1959 double-LP vinyl does not
   contain the between song patter, essential to the full enjoyment of this clas-
   sic. This European release does.
Brewer and Shipley. *Weeds* (Kama Sutra 2016, now packaged with *Tarkio Road*,
      Collector's Choice 461)
*The Bristol Sessions. Historic Recordings from Bristol, Tennessee, featuring the
      First Recordings by the Carter Family, Jimmie Rodgers and Twenty-one
      Additional Artists* (Country Music Foundation CMF11)
The Byrds. *Mr. Tambourine Man* (Sony 64845)
Harry Chapin. *The Bottom Line Encore Collection* (http://harrychapinmusic.
      com)
Classic Folk Music [various artists] (Smithsonian Folkways 40110)
Colors of the Day: The Best of Judy Collins (Elektra/WEA 75030)
The Country Gentlemen. *Folk Songs and Bluegrass* (Smithsonian Folkways
      40022)
Danny Cox. *Sunny* (Pioneer 811P-2125, out-of-print)
Mike Cross. *Live and Kickin'* (Sugar Hill 1005)
Deep River of Song: Black Appalachia. String Bands, Songsters and Hoedowns [var-
      ious artists] (Rounder 1823, download)
An Evening with John Denver (RCA 69353)
Ani DiFranco. *Canon* (Righteous Babe 055)
Donovan. *Live Troubadour* (Great American Music 22)
Don't Mourn—Organize! Songs of Labor Songwriter Joe Hill [various artists]
      (Smithsonian Folkways 40026)
Michael Doucet with Beausoleil. *Parlez-Nous A Boire* (Arhoolie 322)
Antje Duvekot. *The Near Demise of the High Wire Dancer* (Black Wolf Rec-
      ords 8)
Bob Dylan's Greatest Hits (Sony 65975)
Bob Dylan's Greatest Hits, Vol. II (Sony 65976)

The Freewheelin' Bob Dylan (Sony 92396)

Ramblin' Jack Elliott, Spider John Koerner, U. Utah Phillips. *Legends of Folk.*
    (Red House 31)

Fleet Foxes (Sub Pop 777)

Folk Classics. Roots of American Folk Music [various artists] (Columbia 45026,
    download)

Folk Music of Washington Square [various artists] (Smithsonian Folkways 2353)

Friends of Old Time Music: The Folk Arrival 1961–1965 [various artists] (Smith-
    sonian Folkways 40160)

Steve Gillette, Anne Hills, Cindy Mangsen, Michael Smith. *Fourtold* (Appalseed
    1071)

Steve Goodman (SBME Special Markets 724510)

Greatest Folksingers of the 'Sixties [various artists] (Vanguard 17/18)

The Green Fields of America Live in Concert (Compass 4495)

The Greenbriar Boys. *The Best of the Vanguard Years* (Vanguard 206/207)

Nanci Griffith. *One Fair Summer Evening* (MCA 42255)

Arlo Guthrie. *Hobo's Lullaby* (Reprise 2060/Rising Son 2060)

Woody Guthrie. *The Asch Recordings, Vol. 1–4* (Smithsonian Folkways 40112)

The Live Wire: Woody Guthrie in Performance 1949 (Woody Guthrie Founda-
    tion, CD & book)

John Hartford. *Mark Twang* (Flying Fish 20)

Levon Helm. *Dirt Farmer* (Vanguard 79844)

Hootenanny Tonight! [various artists] (Smithsonian Folkways 02511)

Janis Ian. *Folk Is the New Black* (Cooking Vinyl 764)

Ian and Sylvia. *Best of the Vanguard Years* (Vanguard 79516)

The Essential Kingston Trio (Shout Factory 10183)

Leadbelly. *Midnight Special* (Rounder 1044)

Mississippi Sheiks. *Stop and Listen* (Yazoo 2006)

Mud Acres: Music Among Friends [various artists] (Rounder 3001)

Music of Coal: Mining Songs from the Appalachian Coalfields [various artists]
    (Lonesome 071, CD & book)

The New Lost City Ramblers. *50 Years: Where Do You Come From? Where Do You
    Go?* (Smithsonian Folkways 40180)

O Brother, Where Art Thou? [various artists] (Lost Highway 170069)

Phil Ochs. *There But for Fortune* (Elektra 9-60832-1)

Mark O'Connor/Baltimore Symphony Orchestra, Marin Alsop, Conductor.
    Americana Symphony. Variations on Appalachia Waltz (OMAC 12)

Odetta. *Best of the Vanguard Years* (Vanguard 79522)

Our Side of Town: A Red House Records 25th Year Collection [various artists]
    (Red House 210)

Ellis Paul. *Essentials* (Philo 1250)

Tom Paxton. *Live at McCabe's Guitar Shop* (Shout Factory 10085)

Peter, Paul and Mary in Concert (Warner Brothers/WEA 1555)

Robert Plant/Alison Krauss. *Raising Sand* (Rounder 9075)

Ola Belle Reed (Field Recorders' Collective 203)

Jean Ritchie, Oscar Brand, David Sear. *A Folk Concert in Town Hall, New York* (Smithsonian Folkways 2428)

Jean Ritchie and Doc Watson. *At Folk City* (Smithsonian Folkways 40005)

Paul Robeson. *Ballad for Americans* (Vanguard 117/18)

Roots Music. An American Journey [various artists] (Rounder 0501)

Cheapo-Cheapo Productions Presents Real Live John Sebastian (Reprise 2036, reissued Collector's Choice 724)

Pete Seeger. *We Shall Overcome. The Complete Carnegie Hall Concert* (Sony 45312)

Michelle Shocked. *Short Sharp Shocked* (Mighty Sound 1004)

Simon and Garfunkel. *Sounds of Silence* (Sony 65998, expanded)

Rosalie Sorrels/U. Utah Phillips. *The Long Memory* (Red House 83)

Southern Journey. Voices from the American South, Volume 1. Blues, ballads, hymns, reels, shouts, chanteys and work songs. [various artists] (Rounder 1701, download)

Bruce Springsteen. *We Shall Overcome: The Seeger Sessions* (Sony 88231)

Dave Van Ronk. *The Folkways Years 1959–61* (Smithsonian Folkways 40041)

Doc and Merle Watson. *Red Rocking Chair* (Flying Fish 252)

The Weavers at Carnegie Hall (Vanguard 73101)

Robin and Linda Williams. *Buena Vista* (Red House 213)

Woodstock: Music from the Original Soundtrack and More [various artists] (Rhino/WEA 518805)

Woodstock Two [various artists] (Rhino/WEA 518806)

> **Special note:** The climate of the sixties music scene was very open and the music in flux. As a final selection for "Listening Space," check out the dozen or so folk-related tracks on the two volumes from this pivotal festival. Comparing the Woodstock lineup to some of today's more avant-garde rock and, yes, folk festivals, you will discover a lot of similarities. The folk influence continues . . .

Index

About the Author

STEPHANIE P. LEDGIN is an international award-winning photojournalist, whose 35-year career has spanned publications, recordings, and museums. Lincoln Center, Smithsonian Folkways recording label, Country Music Hall of Fame and Museum, and *Sing Out!* magazine, among others, have featured her work. A former New York City radio-show host, she was director of the New Jersey Folk Festival for 10 years. A founding member of Folk Alliance International, she is the author of *Homegrown Music: Discovering Bluegrass* (Praeger, 2004) and *From Every Stage: Images of America's Roots Music* (University Press of Mississippi, 2005). Her Web site is http://fiddlingwithwords.com.